WHAT PEOPLE ARE SAYING ABOUT...

CONNECTED

Katia Adams

Director of Frequentsee and author of Equal
www.frequentsee.org

Connected: God's quiet voice in a world that shouts, is an absolute joy to read. It is beautiful and profound - a feast for your eyes as well as your soul. I found myself regularly nudging my husband to show him images and sentences as I read - this is a book you will want to share as soon as you pick it up.

Angela Kemm

Prophetic Evangelist, Relational Mission & City Church Cambridge

I've enjoyed reading Anna's previous books, so wondered what she'd come up with next. This book doesn't disappoint, it is quite refreshing in its simplicity and yet such a depth of understanding of God and what the human mind perceives and needs. The combination of short teachings and encouragements, together with excellent illustrations, make for a hugely satisfying read. I highly recommend this book to you if you want to grow in your knowledge of God and yourself on a day by day basis.

Some of the material in this manuscript was previously written in the book, "Face to Face. Hearing God's voice for yourself and others".

Cover Design by Daniel Goodman, Dan Gould and Ashley Drew

ISBN 979-864-708-41-70

First Published in 2020 by Amazon
Printed in the United Kingdom

For F.T.O.G. & R.A.E.G.

May the light of Jesus shine through you
as you represent Him to the world around you.

Today you are six and eight.
One day you may become sixty or eighty.
Whatever age you may be,
may you love Jesus with an
outrageous,
audacious,
contagious
love.

Because this is how He loved you first.

A.O.G.G.

WHAT'S INSIDE

WHAT TO EXPECT

PART 1 - GOD CAN SPEAK TO YOU **11**

THE GREAT CONNECTION 12
LISTENING 20
THE BIBLE 54
HOW GOD SPEAKS 72
CONVERSATION 106
A JOURNEY 124

PART 2 - GOD CAN SPEAK THROUGH YOU **147**

WHY DOES HE USE US? 148
HOW DO I SHARE GOD'S HEART? 158
WHEN TO SPEAK 186
THE AFTER PARTY 198
RESPONSIBILITY 216
LIFESTYLE 226

Please engage with this book! There are wide margins so you can write your own thoughts, illustrations and notes. If you feel like God is speaking to you as you read it, write it down so you remember what He's saying. If you're unsure about (or disagree with) something I've written, get out the Bible and test it against what's written there[1]. Don't take me at my word, take God at His.

1 Be like the Bereans! *"Now the Berean Jews were of more noble character than those in Thessalonica, for they received the message with great eagerness and* **examined the Scriptures every day to see if what Paul said was true."** Acts 17:11

FOREWORD

Are you ready?

In Luke 12:35-38, we read a parable that tells us about how we need to be awake and prepared for the soon return of the Master; Jesus. Waiting for our coming King is something we do in an active, not passive, way. As we wait, He wants us to learn about Him, what His voice sounds like, and how we can respond in obedience, out of love, to it.

When I read this book I thought it was amazing. I have never seen a book on the subject of listening and recognising God's voice quite like this - it is unique. I love how practical and easy it is to understand and the beautiful illustrations make the words come alive.

I highly recommend this book to you, it is written for such a time as this.

With love,
Reinhard

Reinhard Hirtler is the founder of Brazilian Kids Kare (www.braziliankidskare.org) and the author of 16 books. He is a church planter, missionary, bible teacher and prophet with 40 years of ministry experience.

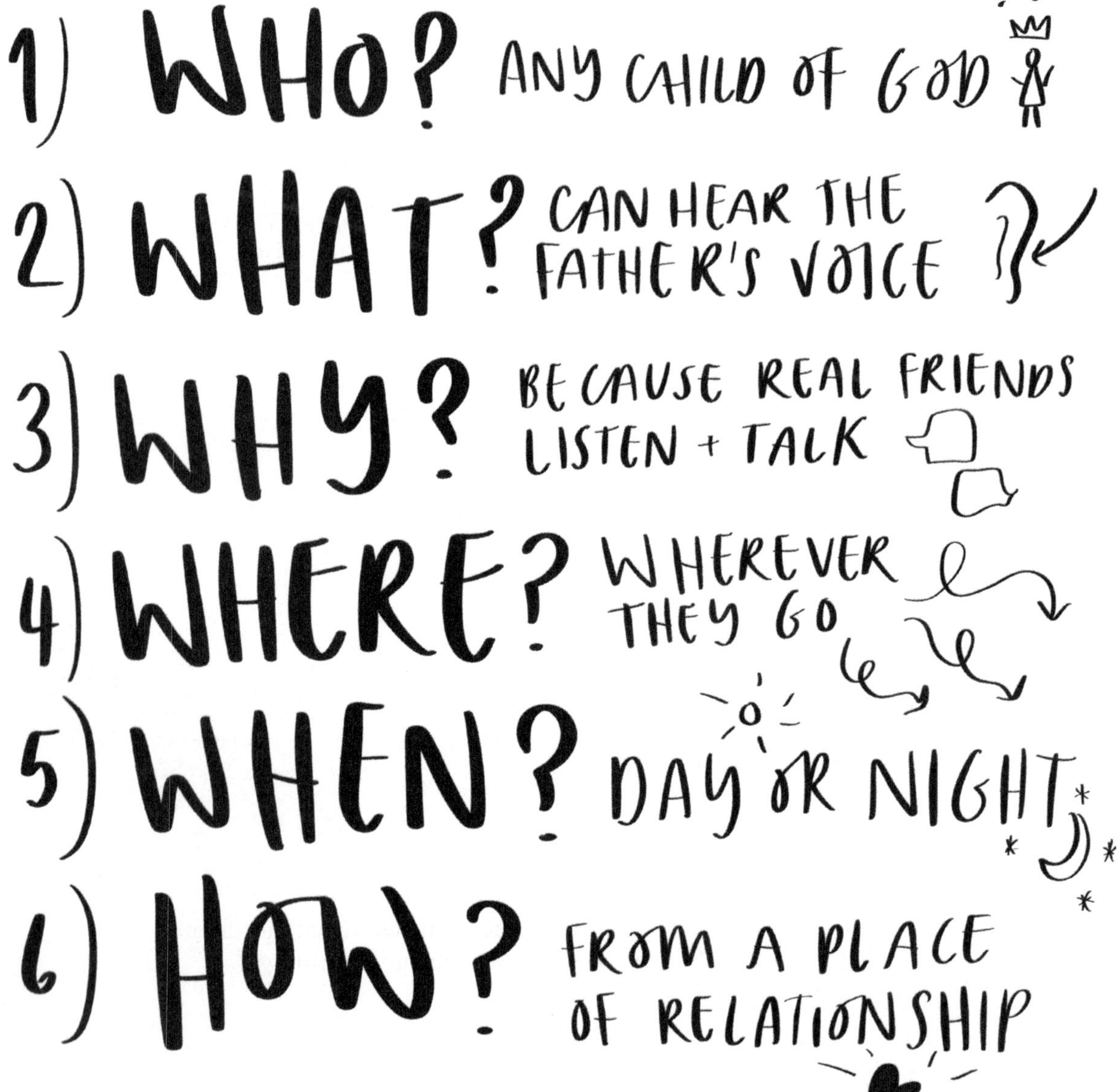
1) WHO? ANY CHILD OF GOD
2) WHAT? CAN HEAR THE FATHER'S VOICE
3) WHY? BECAUSE REAL FRIENDS LISTEN + TALK
4) WHERE? WHEREVER THEY GO
5) WHEN? DAY OR NIGHT
6) HOW? FROM A PLACE OF RELATIONSHIP

INTRODUCTIONS

JESUS, THE WORD

"In the beginning was the Word, and the Word was with God, and the Word was God. He was with God in the beginning. Through him all things were made; without him nothing was made that has been made. In him was life, and that life was the light of all mankind. The light shines in the darkness, and the darkness has not overcome it."

John 1:1-5

Hello!

I want to introduce you to someone.

I don't know if you've met Him before or how well you know Him, but I know He's really looking forward to spending time with you.

His name is Jesus.

If it's ok with you, I'll share some of my story of getting to know Him and what I've learnt along the way. But what I really want is for you to write your own story with Him.

My prayer is that as you read this book, your heart would burn for what's available
to you - a walking, talking relationship with the One who created all things.
He's waiting for you, so let's start walking!

"If you give someone an answer, a rule, a principle, you help them solve one problem. But if you teach them to walk with God, you've helped them solve the rest of their life."

John Eldredge

– PART 1 –

GOD CAN SPEAK TO YOU

LIVING RELATIONSHIPS ARE BUILT ON COMMUNICATION

THE GREAT CONNECTION

YOU WERE CREATED TO COMMUNICATE

We live in a time when we're supposedly more connected to others than ever before. But what has been the cost of that connection? Are we now addicted to approval, desperate to be distracted, fooled by fake news, isolated by iPhone,[1] tempted to troll or constantly comparing?

The bigger question is this: What has this connection done to our *ultimate* connection, to God?

In this chapter we'll begin at the beginning. We'll ask: Who is God? Who are we? What did He do? And why did He do it?

1 Even though we're more connected than ever, a recent study of 55,000 people aged 16+ years found that 40% of respondents aged 16-24 reported feeling lonely often or very often. Young people may be connected, but they are lonely. (https://www.bbc.co.uk/mediacentre/latestnews/2018/loneliest-age-group-radio-4)

CONNECTION

DISCONNECTION

RECONNECTION

THE ORIGINAL PLAN

CREATED FOR RELATIONSHIP

"For he chose us in him before the creation of the world to be holy and blameless in his sight. In love he predestined us for adoption to sonship through Jesus Christ, in accordance with his pleasure and will."
Ephesians 1:4-6

What three words would you use to summarise the entire Bible? Mine would be:

Connection, Disconnection, Reconnection

In Genesis 1 we read how God created humankind in His image in order to have a *relationship*, a friendship, with them. A loving, relational connection was the original intention.

God's children were perfectly, beautifully *connected* to their Creator Father. They were created from love, for love. But God's children decided to do things their own way. They rebelled against The Father and chose to follow their own will instead of God's way.

This rebellion brought a heartbreaking *disconnection* and nothing we could ever do would be able to fix this.

But God The Father had a plan, Jesus - 100% God, 100% man.[1] Through Jesus' birth, death and resurrection, the broken connection between The Father and His children was restored, allowing a *reconnection* of that original relationship for those who believed and accepted Jesus as King of their lives.

Any conversation about hearing from God must begin and end with the love shown to us in Jesus Christ.

IDEA – PRAY

"Jesus, thank you for reconnecting me to the Father."

1 I know this doesn't mathematically make sense, but God isn't limited by our human equations, He is God after all!

FATHERS SPEAK TO THEIR CHILDREN

CHILDREN OF GOD

GOD IS YOUR FATHER

"See what great love the Father has lavished on us, that we should be called children of God! And that is what we are!"
1 John 3:1

If you've given your life to Jesus[1] then Scripture teaches us that Christ's Spirit comes and lives inside of you and that you become adopted (or reconnected) into God's family. You become a child and heir of God, a co-heir with Christ.[2] Isn't that *incredible?*

Most of this world believes that we have to do something in order to *have* something so they can *be* someone.[3] But that's not the Jesus way. You are a child of the loving Father. He is already pleased with you. You do not need to strive for His affection. You do not need to prove anything. This is because of *who He is.* It's about *His* goodness, not ours.

Therefore, when we learn how to rest, confident in the fact that we do not need to earn the right to hear His voice, hearing from God will come more naturally.

Knowing that we are God's children and He is our caring Father should affect everything, and everything we do must come from a place of knowing that we are loved *unconditionally.* When we listen for God's voice it should always sound like a voice of a devoted Father inviting you into a place of deeper relationship with Him.

IDEA – PRAY

"Father God, help me to understand my true identity."

1 Meaning that you've prayed something like this, *"Jesus, I'm sorry for the things I've done wrong in my life. Thank you for dying on the Cross for me, set me free from all my sins and forgive me. Please come into my life and fill me with your Holy Spirit. Be with me forever."*

2 Read Romans 8 if you don't believe me!

3 Hetland, L. (2017) Called to Reign. Living and loving from a place of rest. Convergence Press

mother another mother another
another another another another
another mother another mother
another another another another
mother another mother another
another another another another
another mother another mother
another another another another
mother another mother another
another another another another
another mother another mother
another another another another
mother another mother another
another another another another
another mother another mother
another another another another

CREATED TO COMMUNICATE

YOU WERE DESIGNED TO HEAR GOD'S VOICE

"The sheep listen to his voice. He calls his own sheep by name and leads them out... and his sheep follow him because they know his voice."
John 10:3-4

You were created to hear God's voice.

Imagine if you had kids one day. How likely would it be that you would stand in front of them without saying a word? Of course you wouldn't do that!

Being a child of God means that you are like God's sheep and will therefore *'know His voice.'* In other words, being God's sheep qualifies you to hear the voice of Jesus, The Good Shepherd. Not only does it qualify you, but God actually *desires* to talk to you, His child, in an ongoing way![1]

Research has shown that even in the womb a baby can distinguish between the voice of her mother over the voice of another.[2] The baby's heart beats faster in response to the one who will bring them into the world and care for them.

God is our Father and we too can expect this kind of connection with Him.

Jeremiah 1:5 says, *"Before I formed you in the womb I knew you".* This also applies to you. Before your parents knew you existed, God knew you. You were alive in His heart. He was speaking His words over you right from the beginning.

IDEA – PRAY

"Jesus, please help me recognise Your voice more clearly."

1 Zephaniah 3:7 says, *"He takes great delight in you and rejoices over you with singing!"*

2 Queen's University. *"Fetus Heart Races When Mom Reads Poetry; New Findings Reveal Fetuses Recognize Mother's Voice In-utero."* ScienceDaily. ScienceDaily, 13 May 2003.

LISTENING

CONNECTING TO GOD'S HEART IN A WORLD OF DISTRACTION

When we talk to God:

1. We need to *listen* and *look.*
2. We need to *see* and *hear.*
3. We need to *understand.*
4. We need to *act.*

We will begin to look at out how we can listen and look, see and hear God's voice. It might sound like a really basic first step, but simple doesn't always mean easy.

"Son of man, all my words that I shall speak to you receive in your heart, and hear with your ears."

Ezekiel 3:10 (ESV)

I DID NOTHING

I STOPPED...

I WAITED...

I STOPPED...

I WAITED...

I LISTENED...

SUPERMARKET LIVES

IN A NOISY WORLD WE NEED TO INTENTIONALLY LISTEN

"A large crowd followed and pressed around him."
Mark 5:24

A while ago I went to the supermarket with my husband and two sons to pick up a few items. It was immediately apparent that we'd chosen the wrong hour of the wrong day because the supermarket was heaving with driven, mid-morning shoppers. It was an overwhelming and unpleasant experience which became worse when I discovered that somehow, at some point, I'd managed to lose my husband and both unimpressed children.[1] Despite my earnest efforts, I simply could not find them, the chaos was too intense and the shoppers were too dense.

What would you have done? Summoned them over the tannoy? Climbed on top of the World Food shelves hoping your bird's eye view would give you an excellent vantage point?

I decided to do nothing.

I just stopped right there in the middle of Aisle No. 8 and waited. I stopped and I waited and I listened. And then do you know what happened? Once I'd managed to filter out some of the background noise and chatter, very faintly in the distance I recognised the voice of my youngest son trying to convince my husband to buy doughnuts. So, I focused on his voice and followed his words until they became clearer and eventually there he was.

Sometimes our busy 'supermarket lives' can get very noisy and full. Our challenge in listening to God's voice is to take the time to *stop* and be *still;* to *wait, minimise distractions* and *focus,* to *recognise, follow* and *draw near* to the God who is calling out our name.

IDEA – ASK

God to help you focus on His voice even when you're surrounded by noise & distraction.

1 You'll notice a theme with a lot of the stories I tell - many of them include my children. This is intentional. As often as possible, I want to remind you of your relationship with God, you are His child, He is your Father.

PEACE
+
CALM

GALE FORCE WIND AND DESTRUCTION

GALE FORCE WIND

AND DESTRUCTION

GALE FORCE WIND

AND DESTRUCTION

GALE FORCE WIND

AND DESTRUCTION

GALE FORCE WIND

AND DESTRUCTION

GALE FORCE WIND

AND DESTRUCTION

BE STILL

BE STILL

BE STILL

QUIET HEARTS HEAR GOD

"But I have calmed and quieted myself"
Psalm 131:2

My two sons are more like lion cubs – they constantly roll around on top of one another. They also don't have a volume dial – either they're asleep or they're roaring. I remember one morning being in my kitchen whilst every pot and pan was being drummed on when I felt God speak into my heart, *"Be still".*

My 'holy' response was to complain: 'What an unfair thing to ask of me! Couldn't God see what I was dealing with?' (At that precise moment I was trying to prevent my cat from being forced into the washing machine.) How I longed to sit in a dark corner somewhere in stillness!

But then a quiet reply entered my mind, *"The kind of stillness I need you to learn is in your heart".*

Then I remembered something. In my childhood, I lived in the West Indies[1] and during the summer months we'd often get hurricane warnings. I felt God reminded me about this in order to show me something. The outside of a hurricane is where all of the gale force winds are that cause destruction.[2] However in the centre, or eye, of the storm there is peace and quiet.

The winds of life will blow at different strengths at different times in our life. We won't always be able to change that. But what we can do is to learn how to regularly enter into the calm and peace of God's presence, intentionally stilling our hearts before Him.

Even in a storm you can choose to be still.

IDEA – DO

Spend 20 minutes intentionally trying to quieten your heart.

---

1 My father was a tropical forest consultant. His work meant we lived in Honduras, Nepal, Belgium, Barbados and Great Britain.

2 Not unlike my children.

CALM

HAILSTONES

HEART POSTURE

STILLING YOURSELF CAN BE DONE ANYWHERE

"He makes me lie down in green pastures. He leads me beside still waters."
Psalm 23:2 (ESV)

Listening for God can be like looking for reflections on the surface of a river. When a river is calm, the reflections of what's projected onto it are easier to identify. In contrast, attempting to see the reflections on a river during a hailstorm is almost impossible.

This is what we're trying to do – we're trying to still our heart's 'river' so we can see what God is trying to show us more clearly and sometimes it takes time to wait whilst the ripples subside.

Stilling your heart can be done while sitting, running, dancing, lying down or driving – it isn't the position of the body that matters but the posture of the heart. You can have a 'noisy heart' when you're by yourself and a 'still heart' whilst sitting on a crowded bus.

There's a path I can take around our village that lasts about an hour and that's when I spend my intentional time connecting to God. It takes me 8,937 steps and during that time, whilst I'm briskly walking, I'm also actually at my most still.

Listening to God is more than simply sitting in silence, it's about stilling the heart.

IDEA – THINK

Where and when are you at your most still?

Spend time there.

IT'S HARDER TO HEAR

RELAX & REST

WE DON'T NEED TO STRIVE TO HEAR GOD

"Come with me by yourselves to a quiet place and get some rest."
Mark 6:31

I wonder what you're like under pressure. Do you thrive and come alive or do you fry like an egg in the sun? Sometimes when I'm under stress my brain seems to freeze and body seems to seize.

Being stressed affects your ability to hear.[1] I once listened to a talk about how to hear God's voice and was intrigued by the fact that it was all about being too stressed.

What applies in our bodies also applies in our soul - being stressed makes it harder to hear from God.

Isaiah 40:31 says, *"but those who hope in the Lord will renew their strength. They will soar on wings like eagles; they will run and not grow weary, they will walk and not be faint."*

Sometimes I ask myself, *"Am I soaring or am I flapping?"* When we learn how to rest, confident in the fact that we do not need to strive to earn the right to hear His voice, hearing from God will come more naturally.

IDEA – READ

John 8:47 "Whoever belongs to God hears what God says."

Rest and digest these words.

1 Stress disturbs blood circulation throughout the body. When your body responds to stress, the overproduction of adrenaline reduces blood flow to the ears, affecting hearing.

OKAY GOOGLE
WHAT IS...?

INSTANT
ANSWER

HEY SIRI
HOW DOES..?

INSTANT
RESPONSE

ALEXA
WHEN IS..?

INSTANT
REPLY

WAIT PATIENTLY

HEARING FROM GOD IS NOT AN 'ON-DEMAND' SERVICE

"Be still before the Lord and wait patiently for him"
Psalm 37:7

We live in an instant world and God is not a vending machine. Our tolerance for waiting is limited, but God is in no hurry.

If we want to contact someone we can send them an email or message on our phone and know that the recipient will almost instantly receive it. If we want to know what the current population of Honduras is, we can type or ask Google, Alexa or Siri and get an answer within seconds. Our expectation is that of immediacy.[1]

When talking to our Heavenly Father, we need to remember that He may have a different time frame to ours.

Think about one of your best friends for a moment - when are they allowed to talk to you? Is it only at lunchtime between 12.30-1.00pm? No, of course not. You try to make yourself available to them as often as possible.

Why is it that we sometimes try to time-restrict God? We (may) have our dedicated time of prayer and study and assume that if He's going to talk to us, He has to do it then. But God doesn't want boxes or limits. He wants to have conversations with you, answer your questions and reveal things to you, but He wants to do that without restriction, just like a friend.

If you don't feel like you're hearing from Him as soon as you've started praying, don't assume God doesn't have anything to say to you or that you're not listening 'well enough'. God can talk to you in any given moment. Be expectant, keep waiting patiently.

IDEA – DO

Spend time waiting expectantly for God to speak.

Don't rush.

1 Interesting fact: According to the Nielsen Norman Group who market themselves as "World Leaders in Research-Based User Experience" the average internet page visit lasts a little less than a minute and web users often leave in just 10–20 seconds.

IT'S HARDER TO HEAR GOD'S VOICE WHEN YOU ALLOW OTHER PEOPLE'S VOICES TO BE LOUDER THAN GOD'S

NOISE & DISTRACTION

MINIMISE OBSTACLES

"But Martha was distracted"
Luke 10:40

My husband and I were both brought up in the tropics. As a result of living in the heat, we both used to sleep with a fan on. Many years later and now living in Britain, we both still sleep with a fan – even in winter. The white noise comforts us!

We used to live in a 130-year-old house and once we had a power cut. At first I really struggled to sleep - the silence was deafening. However, as I adjusted to the quiet, I then couldn't sleep because I realised how *noisy* our old house was! I started to hear creaks, whistles and groans of the windows, floorboards and chimney that I'd never heard before because the fan masked it.

This can be the same when learning to recognise God's voice. At first you may feel uncomfortable with the silence and the waiting, but as you learn to filter out your internal brain chatter, you'll realise that God isn't as silent as you may have thought.[1]

I've noticed that certain things (e.g. social media) create extra noise in my head.[2] Having the voices of so many other people echoing inside my mind makes it more difficult to be receptive to God's voice.[3]

It's hard to hear God's voice when we allow other people's voices to be louder than His. The solution isn't asking God to speak louder, but for us to become quieter.

IDEA – THINK

What one step can you take today to minimise the noise and distraction in your life?

1 *"It's not the chatter of people around us that is the most powerful distractor, but rather the chatter of our own minds."* Daniel Goleman

2 Even if I was on social media for just five minutes, the residual conversations remained rattling inside my head for much longer.

3 It makes me sad to think that God may have attempted to talk to me on many occasions but I somehow drowned Him out.

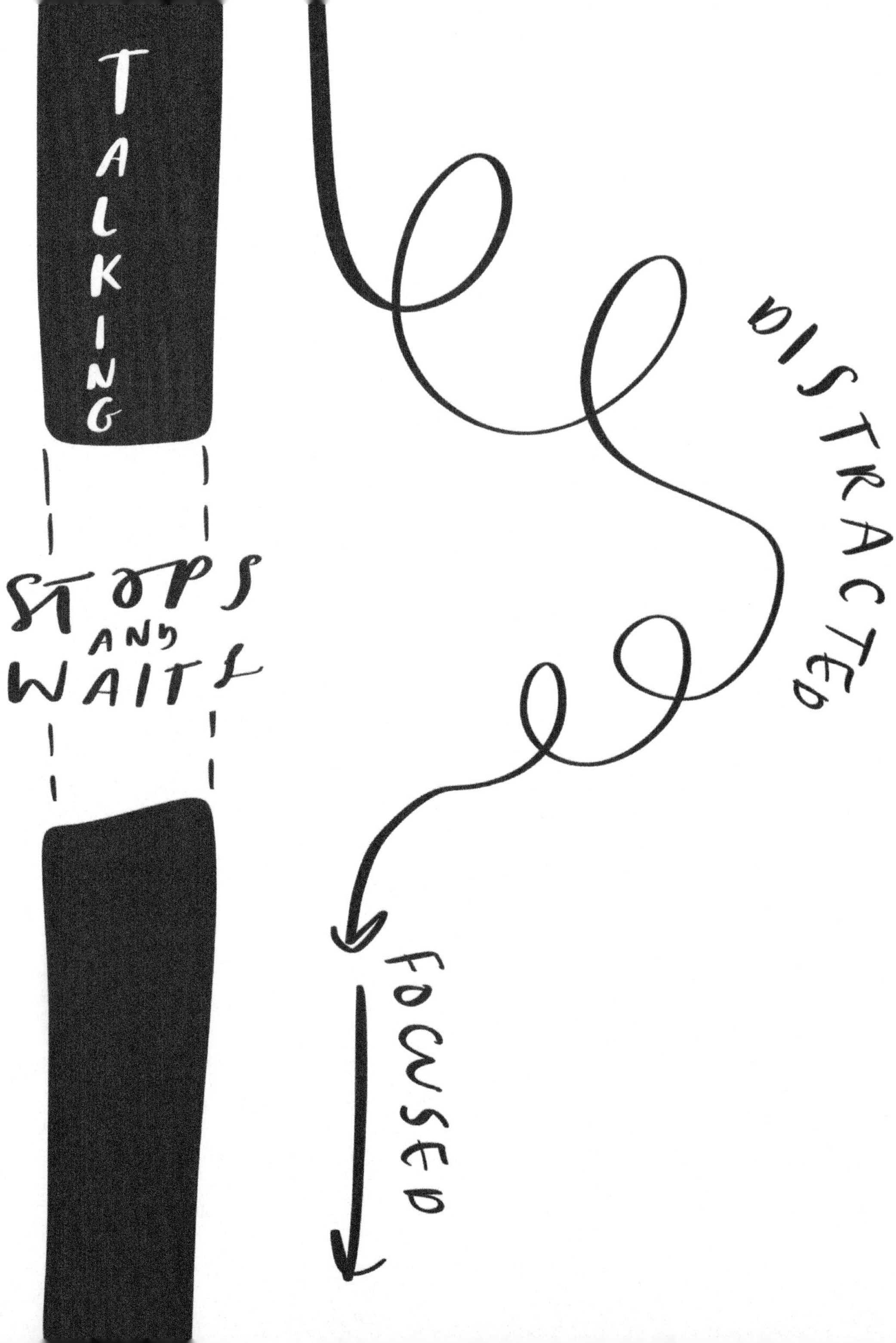

TALKING

STOPS AND WAITS

DISTRACTED

FOCUSED

A RAIN DROP

FOCUSING OUR ATTENTION ON GOD

"Set your minds on things above, not on earthly things."
Colossians 3:2

Pete Greig provoked me with his comment, *"Satan's primary objective has never been to tempt you into violating a particular set of rules. His number one aim is simply to divert your attention away from Jesus. He'll use sin to do it, for sure. But he'll equally use busyness or Candy Crush Saga."*[1]

What, or who, has your attention?
Pay attention to what has your attention.

When I'm having a conversation with my eldest son, sometimes he goes silent. He stops talking because he can tell that I'm distracted and doesn't want to continue until my eyes are focused back on him. He knows that when I give him eye contact, I'm more likely to really hear what he has to say.

So he waits until he has my attention, my undivided attention.

If a single rain drop were to fall on you, would you notice it? If you're busy and distracted, a drop could land on you and you might not feel it. If, however, you have stilled yourself and you are consciously waiting for the rain drop to fall, you'll be aware of it when it does.

When we live a life with a conviction and expectation that our God can speak to us at any time, it will help us recognise those moments when they happen.

We honour God when we give Him our full attention.[2]

IDEA – THINK

What one change can you make today to help you focus more on God?

1 Greig, P. (2018) Dirty Glory: Go where your best prayers take you, Hodder & Stoughton.

2 Some believe that the average human attention span is continually decreasing. The Statistic Brain Research Institute reported in 2000 that the average attention span was 12 seconds. Fifteen years later it had decreased to 8.25 seconds, which is less than that of a goldfish (9 seconds)!

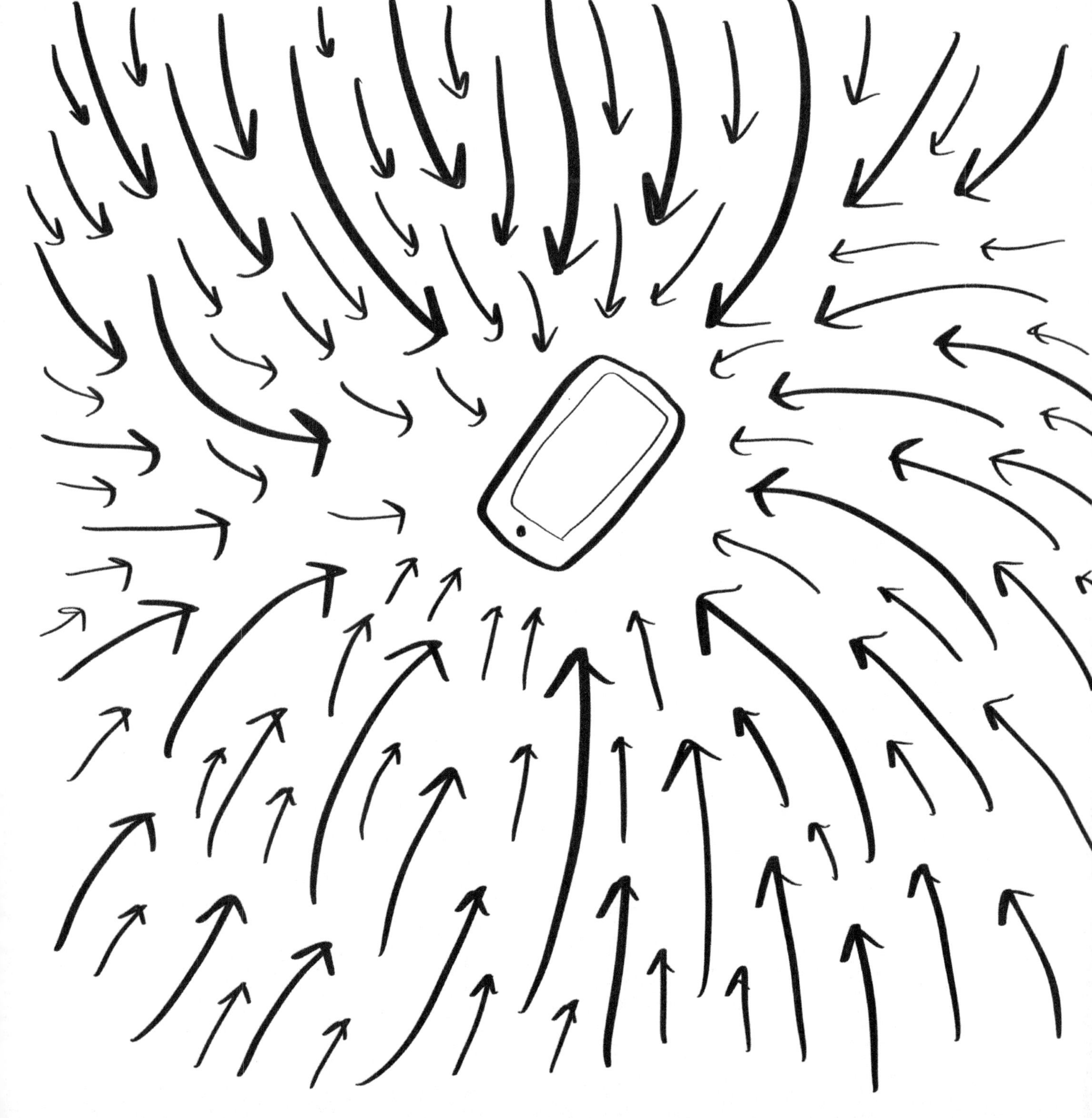

DISCONNECT

SWITCH OFF FROM TECHNOLOGY

"But Jesus often withdrew to lonely places and prayed."
Luke 5:16

FOMO or *"Fear Of Missing Out"* is an often used term. One could argue that we've become a society that is so worried about missing out on the latest bit of information that we've become unhealthily attached to technology. The average person picks up their smartphone 221 times a day (totalling on average three hours and 16 minutes).[1]

I wonder how that compares to how much time we intentionally connect with God?

Any kind of technology can be a wonderful, powerful tool when it's used in its proper place. But it can also be an obstacle when trying to connect with God if it robs you of your attention and affection.

I read this recently: *"In a meeting or a classroom, if my phone is away, I am more likely to be perceived as engaged. If my phone is not in use, but is face up on the table, I present myself as engaged for the moment, but possibly disengaged if someone more important outside the room needs me. And if my phone is in my hand, and I am responding to texts and scrolling social media, I project open dismissiveness.*[2]*"*

Often, saying *"yes"* to one thing means saying *"no"* to another. If you want to say *"yes"* to connecting with God, it will mean saying *"no"* to connecting with other things.

Be aware of what you're saying *"yes"* and *"no"* to.

IDEA – DO

Plan a phone fast.

Spend the whole day with your phone switched off.

1 According to research carried out by Tecmark on 2,000 smartphone users. https://www.tecmark.co.uk/blog/smartphone-usage-data-uk-2014

2 Reinke, T (2017). 12 Ways your phone is changing you. Illinois: Crossway.

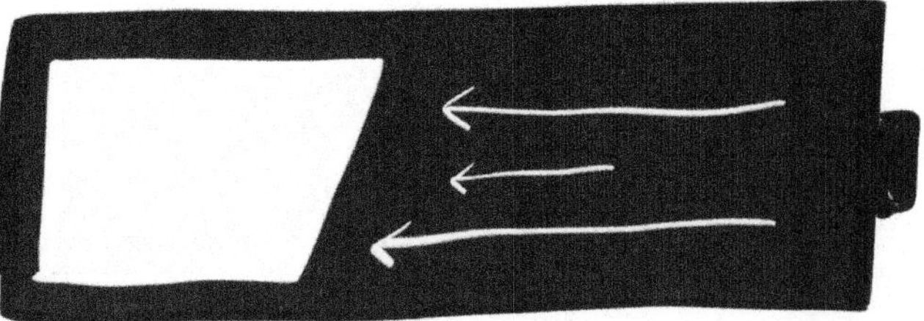

SELF AWARE

GIVE GOD YOUR BEST

"Very early in the morning, while it was still dark, Jesus... prayed."
Mark 1:35

My phone is several years old. As soon as I turn it on the battery starts to go down. If I open any of my apps, the battery drains faster. If I use Google Maps then I guarantee you my phone will go from 98% to 0% battery in under three minutes.[1] I know this about my phone and so if I need to make a phone call, I know I need to do this as the beginning of the day when my battery is at its best.

I'm a bit like my phone. As soon as I'm around (most) people, my internal battery starts to drain. I'm also not great at multi-tasking or multi-thinking. When I've got more things going on in my life, it's like I have more 'background apps' open in my brain. These take up energy even when I'm not actively engaged with them.[2]

The point I'm trying to make is this: *Be self-aware.*

Know when you're at your best in terms of your energy. God deserves you at your *best,* not when you're about to run out of battery and switch off mid sentence. You're also more likely to hear God's voice when you are at your most alert and focused and not just about to fall asleep.

For me, this means that if I want to have a decent amount of time with God, I need to do that at the beginning of the day, not at the end. It also helps me get in tune with God's agenda for the day (like you'd tune your instrument before, not after, an orchestra performance).

IDEA – REFLECT

When are you at your best?

Give some of this time to God.

1 This is highly inconvenient, especially when you're stuck in the middle of an English country lane in the dark with cows rubbing up against your car.

2 For example, tonight we have a group of people coming over for an hour. Even though they're going to be there for only one hour, just *knowing* that they're coming later has taken up a bit of my mental capacity *all day*.

HUMBLE YOURSELF

IT'S A PRIVILEGE TO SPEAK TO GOD

"Since the first day that you set your mind to gain understanding and to humble yourself before your God, your words were heard."
Daniel 10:12

In the Old Testament we read about how once a year, one single man, a High Priest, was allowed into the Holy of Holies to stand before God on behalf of the people. He had to do very specific things in a very specific way and wear very specific clothing in order to come out alive. It was probably a terrifying experience to come before a Holy, Holy God. The High Priest was a mediator, foreshadowing the ultimate High Priest and mediator, Jesus.

Because Jesus took our sins upon Himself, we can now come before Our Holy Father and talk to Him directly. This is such a privilege. In a world where a sense of entitlement underlies much of what is expected, it's important that we keep our hearts humble. God owes us nothing. He gave us everything. Coming before Him is an incredible privilege.

I was at St. Andrews University in my final year when Prince William started his first year.[1] I remember bumping into him several times[2] and each time I felt a bit awestruck because of his royal status. How much more overwhelmed should I feel each time I come before God? The fact that I should be given the personal attention of the King of Kings should fill me with great reverence and fear - it shouldn't ever be something that I take for granted.

IDEA – REFLECT

When you pray, is it with humility?

Are you aware you're speaking to the King of Kings?

1 Note, I was there first! Apparently St. Andrews had a 44% increase in applications once people found out he was going there (https://www.theguardian.com/education/2001/jan/26/highereducation.news). Well, I wasn't one of them!

2 I almost trod on his foot once, by mistake.

EARS TO HEAR

LISTENING WELL[1]

"But blessed are your eyes because they see, and your ears because they hear."
Matthew 13:16

There are certain songs I love. I love them so much, in fact, that I've lost count of how many times I've listened to them. But I can assure you I know them inside out. Then my husband will come along and say, *"that line is just ridiculous"* or *"it's such a sad story".*

And I won't have a clue what he's talking about.

I've been listening to the melody, not to the words. I've heard how the song makes me *feel,* but not what the song is actually *saying.* Because my husband is a songwriter, he listens to the lyrics. I don't. It's a whole different layer to the song that I've never actually truly heard before, even though it's been there all along.

My listening has been superficial and limited.

When we're listening to God's voice, there's often a tune and a message. We need to listen for both.

IDEA – PRAY

"Father God, help me to learn how to really listen to your voice. I don't want to miss out on any of your words."

1 My husband often wisely says, *"Listen with your ears, not with your mouth!"*

A A

EYES TO SEE

LOOKING PROPERLY

"I will look to see what he will say to me"
Habakkuk 2:1

My husband, Daniel, loves typefaces and fonts (except Comic Sans) and he notices letters.[1] I remember one frosty morning walking down the old quaint streets of Ely, when all of a sudden Daniel stopped and abruptly turned around. He then briskly marched back to a shop we'd just passed and whipped out his camera. My puzzled expression must have been evident because he felt the need to elaborate.

He said with great passion: *"Look! What's wrong with that sign?!"* I studied it, calmly at first, but then with an edge of panic as I struggled to see anything of relevance. I had no idea what I was supposed to be looking at. Eventually I gave up.

"Focus on the first A, then look at the second one - it's vertically flipped. That 100-year-old sign has one of its 'A's back-to-front!"

Once he'd pointed it out to me, it *was* obvious.

Often my children will be looking for something, declare it lost forever, only for me to find it three minutes later (usually somewhere right in front of their noses). They would look, but not see. Using your 'Mummy eyes' is therefore an expression we use to look differently and see what's there but not being currently seen.

When we intentionally learn to look and see, we start to *become aware* of things that God is trying to show us which have been there all along, yet have not actually been seen. We therefore need to ask God to help us see with His eyes.

IDEA – READ

2 Kings 6.

THEN PRAY

"Open my eyes, LORD, so that I may see."

1 He studied graphic design at university.

SOMETIMES GOD'S VOICE
IS SO FAMILIAR YOU
THINK IT'S YOUR THOUGHTS

VOICE RECOGNITION

GOD'S VOICE CAN BE EASILY IGNORED

"Then the Lord called Samuel. Samuel answered, "Here I am." And he ran to Eli and said, "Here I am; you called me."
1 Samuel 3:4

God's voice is easy to dismiss.

In the book of 1 Samuel we read how God calls Samuel three times but Samuel keeps thinking it's Eli. Although he *hears* God's voice, he doesn't *recognise* it as belonging to God. It's only when Eli realises that God is speaking to Samuel that he's able to explain that and Samuel is then able to say, *"Speak, Lord, for your servant is listening"* (1 Samuel 3:10).

I believe God is talking more than we realise, we just don't recognise it's Him.[1]

Did you know that many of the Jews in the Bible rejected Jesus as their Saviour because He didn't look the way they thought a Saviour should?

So often we miss what God is saying because we expect Him to talk in a certain way or to sound completely different than any voice we've ever heard before. One might expect a booming voice, lightning to flash and for angels to sing, but often His voice is a gentle whisper that could be, and is, easily ignored.

IDEA – REFLECT

God's voice may sound so familiar to you that you think it's your own thoughts.

1 We were created to recognise and respond to God's voice and we're promised that we will not follow the voice of a stranger (John 10:5). But we aren't promised that there will be no other voices. There are lots of voices that we will hear in our mind. Our own voices, other's voices, God's voice and even sometimes the enemy's voice saying things to us that we could think are our own thoughts. It's therefore important that we recognise the *difference* between all the voices and that often takes *experience*. The Holy Spirit can help us with this and show us which voices belong to another and which belong to God.

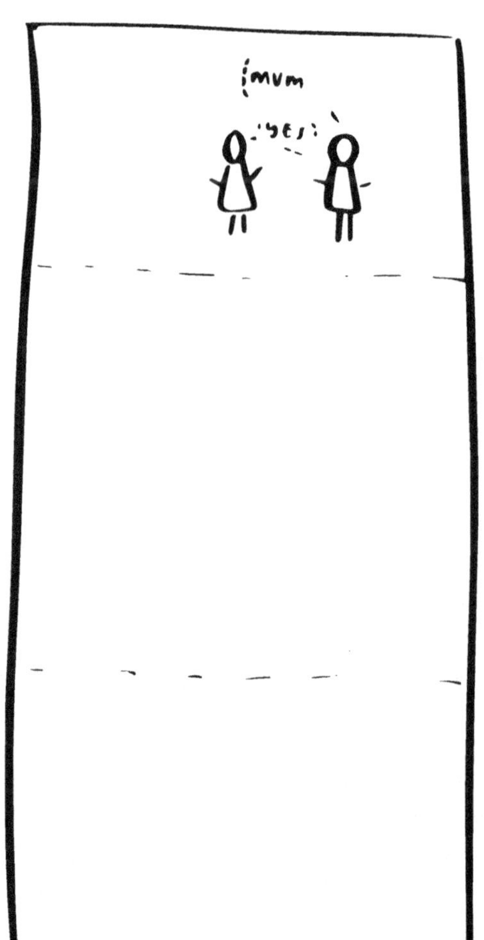

I WANT THEM TO COME CLOSER – SO WE CAN HAVE A CONVERSATION

DRAW NEAR

GOD WANTS YOU TO COME CLOSE TO HIM

"Draw near to God and He'll draw near to you"
James 4:8

We live in a three-storey house. Often, much to my despair, if one of my boys wants to ask me something whilst they're on the ground floor and I'm on the top floor, instead of walking up the two flights of stairs to speak to me, they'll just yell.

LOUDLY.

I'm not a fan of being yelled at. I'm also not a fan of needing to yell back to someone in order to reply. Neither are my neighbours. So what I do is make them come upstairs to ask me their question.

I want them to come closer to me so we can have a conversation.

If you wanted to whisper something to someone, how close would they have to be to you in order to hear what you're saying?

Very close, right?

I think that's why God often chooses to speak quietly[1]. So we have to come close to Him in order to hear His words properly.

God loves it when we take the time to draw near to Him. When we draw near, He draws near.

IDEA – DO

Put an empty seat next to you and imagine God sitting there.

What would you say to Him?

1 We'll discuss this more in the next chapter.

AGAIN
AGAIN
AGAIN!

KNOW & ENJOY

GOD WANTS A MEANINGFUL FRIENDSHIP

"Be still, and know that I am God"
Psalm 46:10

You're in the reception area of your doctor's surgery waiting to be called in for your appointment. There are four other people with you and there's a 45-minute delay. Silently you wait, willing the next name to be yours. Fifty minutes later you're summoned, have your appointment and leave.

Now let me ask you a question. How well do you know any of the four people that you waited with for 45 minutes? Do you know any of their names, occupations, concerns, hopes or future plans? Probably not. Why? Because being in someone's presence is not the same as knowing them, having fellowship and companionship with them.

Getting to know God better means you'll recognise His voice more easily when He speaks. This takes some investment.

When my children were young their favourite game was *"Catch you!"* It's not complicated. They run and you run after them in hot pursuit (but not too fast). When the shrieks and anticipation levels have reached a peak, you catch them. And they *loved* it! The thrill of the chase, the anticipation of being caught, the delight in the catch itself - the whole thing brought so much joy they'd always ask for more.

Our Father loves to be the focus of our attention. God doesn't want you to talk to Him only when you have an underlying agenda or request, He wants you to simply enjoy being with Him, just like you would with a friend.

And it's from a place of friendship that God loves to share His heart and thoughts with us.

IDEA – READ

Jeremiah 29:13

"You will seek me and find me, when you seek me with all your heart."

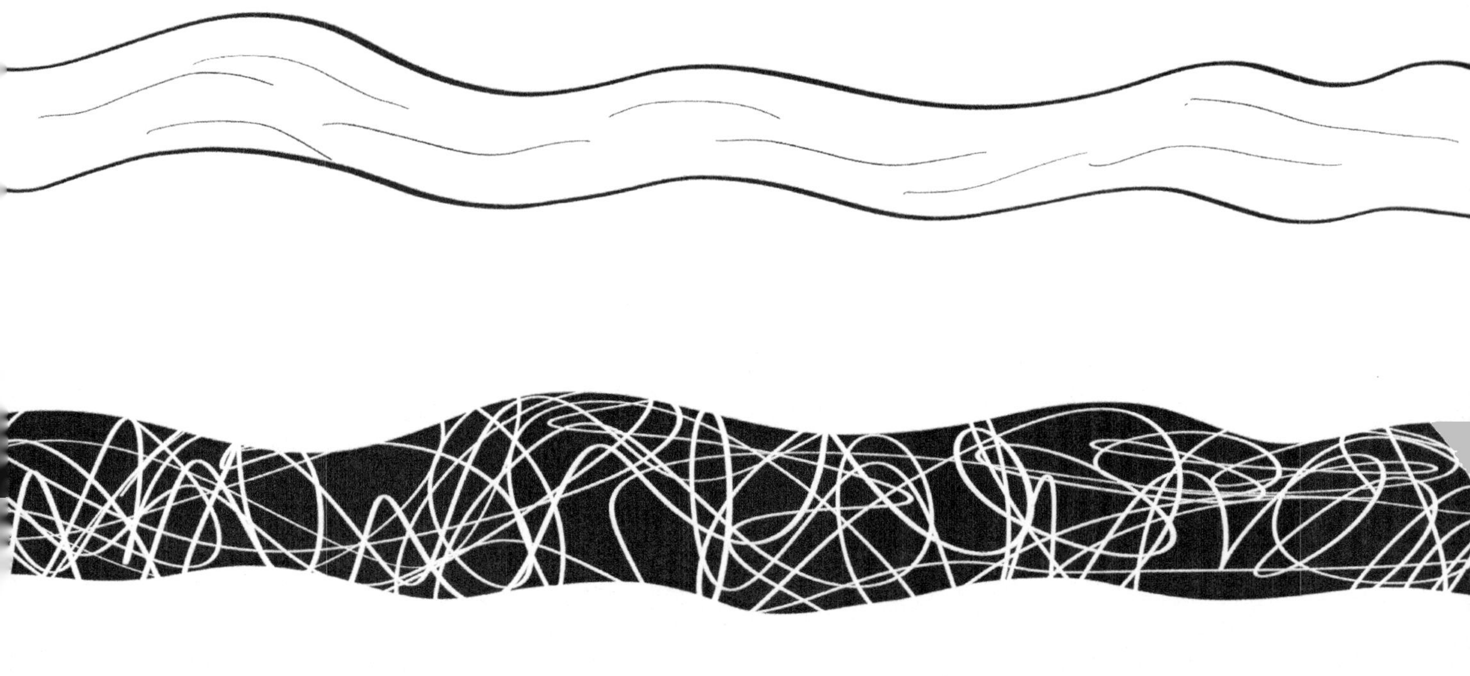

WHICH RIVER WOULD YOU CHOOSE?

HOLY CHANNELS

PURE HEARTS SEE GOD

"The eye is the lamp of the body. If your eyes are healthy, your whole body will be full of light."
Matthew 6:22

God is holy so we must live holy lives.

My grandmother is Swiss. Up in the Alps, the streams are a glistening, pure turquoise. The sunlight twinkles on the surface and the water is so clear it's like looking through glass. Now consider a slow-flowing, murky river, so dense with algae and pollution that only parasitic life survives. Imagine being told there are gold nuggets at the bottom of both rivers, if you can find them. Both have gold, both just as deep.

Which river would you choose?

Sin is like pollution that brings distortion. It affects our ability to see the precious things of God. Jesus says, *"Blessed are the pure in heart for they will see God."*[1] If we want to see what God is seeing and saying, then keeping our hearts and minds pure will help us do that.

Psalm 119:37 says, *"Turn my eyes away from worthless things."* I used to love reading and watching meaningless rubbish, even though I knew it was mental junk food. However, I was reminded that we're channels for God's Spirit to flow through. Everything we expose ourselves to has an effect on us, just in the same way as pouring something into a river has. I now try to be careful about the things I listen to and watch.

The clearer the river, the easier it is to see God's gold.

IDEA – REFLECT

Is there anything I need to change to live a purer life?

1 See Matthew 5:8. Also read Philippians 4:8 *"Whatever is true, whatever is noble, whatever is right, whatever is pure, whatever is lovely, whatever is admirable – if anything is excellent or praiseworthy – think about such things."*

THE BIBLE

CONNECTED TO GOD'S WRITTEN WORD

The Bible is God's inspired words that He has already spoken and by the Holy Spirit He continues to speak through them.

Connecting to God's written word helps us know God's heart more and keeps us (and others) safe and grounded in truth.

THE ULTIMATE DIARY

SCRIPTURE HELPS US KNOW GOD BETTER

"All Scripture is God-breathed and is useful for teaching, rebuking, correcting and training in righteousness, so that the servant of God may be thoroughly equipped for every good work."
2 Timothy 3: 16-17

The Bible is God's inspired written word.

Think about someone in history you really admire - perhaps it's Nelson Mandela, Neil Armstrong or Mother Teresa. Now imagine that they gave you their personal diary and invited you to read it. Would you?

That's a bit like how I see the Bible - as God's diary. The ultimate diary. I think it's an incredible privilege to have access to His inspired word. Just like any other diary, it contains facts, feelings, conversations, reactions, plans, hopes, dreams, stories etc. And just like you'd expect from reading someone else's diary, it helps us get to know the author of the words better and to love Him more.

The Bible is given to us to help us grow in our relationship and love of God.

The more we read the Bible, the more we know who God is and what His character and nature is like. What He loves and hates. It helps us to understand His mind. Our knowledge of the Bible should cause us to hunger for God, to fall more in love with Him, worship Him more, and grow more eagerly in our desire to share the love of God with other people.[1]

IDEA - REFLECT

How often do you read the Bible?

Is it important to you?

1 We read the Bible *not* to EARN (it doesn't justify you), but to 1. LEARN (about God, world, ourselves), 2. DISCERN (it shapes our thinking which leads to wisdom), 3. TURN (it causes repentance), 4. BURN (it sets our heart on fire) and 5. YEARN (for heaven on earth). (For more detail, read this by Andrew Wilson: https://think-theology.co.uk/blog/article/why_do_we_read_scripture.)

TRUTH

THE TRUTH

THE ULTIMATE SOURCE OF TRUTH IS THE BIBLE

"For the word of God is alive and active. Sharper than any double-edged sword, it penetrates even to dividing soul and spirit, joints and marrow; it judges the thoughts and attitudes of the heart."
Hebrews 4:12

Fake news, it's everywhere. What's trustworthy, what's false? The information available to us these days can be so easily fabricated, twisted and manipulated. And the disturbing thing is that we're easily fooled by fake news and we don't always care, as long as it's entertaining.

I've noticed something that has really concerned me. Absolute truth no longer seems important in our society, what matters is 'your truth'. It seems that something is true if it's true to you and that's what really counts.

This is *not* true! Christians believe that the *ultimate source of truth* is the Bible. We measure everything against it. Anything that contradicts what God has clearly written in His Word should be rejected.

Whenever we feel like we are hearing from God we must remember we're still fallible. We will be limited in the way we perceive, understand and interpret what we think He's saying. Anything revealed to us outside of the Bible does not therefore carry that same level of infallible, Scripture-level authority. Scripture is closed and final, nothing can be added to it. It's a foundation, not a building process.

Whatever we hear, should be tested against what's written in the Bible.[1] Remaining connected to God's written Word will protect us from anything false.

IDEA – PRAY

"Thank you Jesus that we can know the Truth"

1 But in order to do this, we first need to know what's written in the Bible. We do this by reading it!

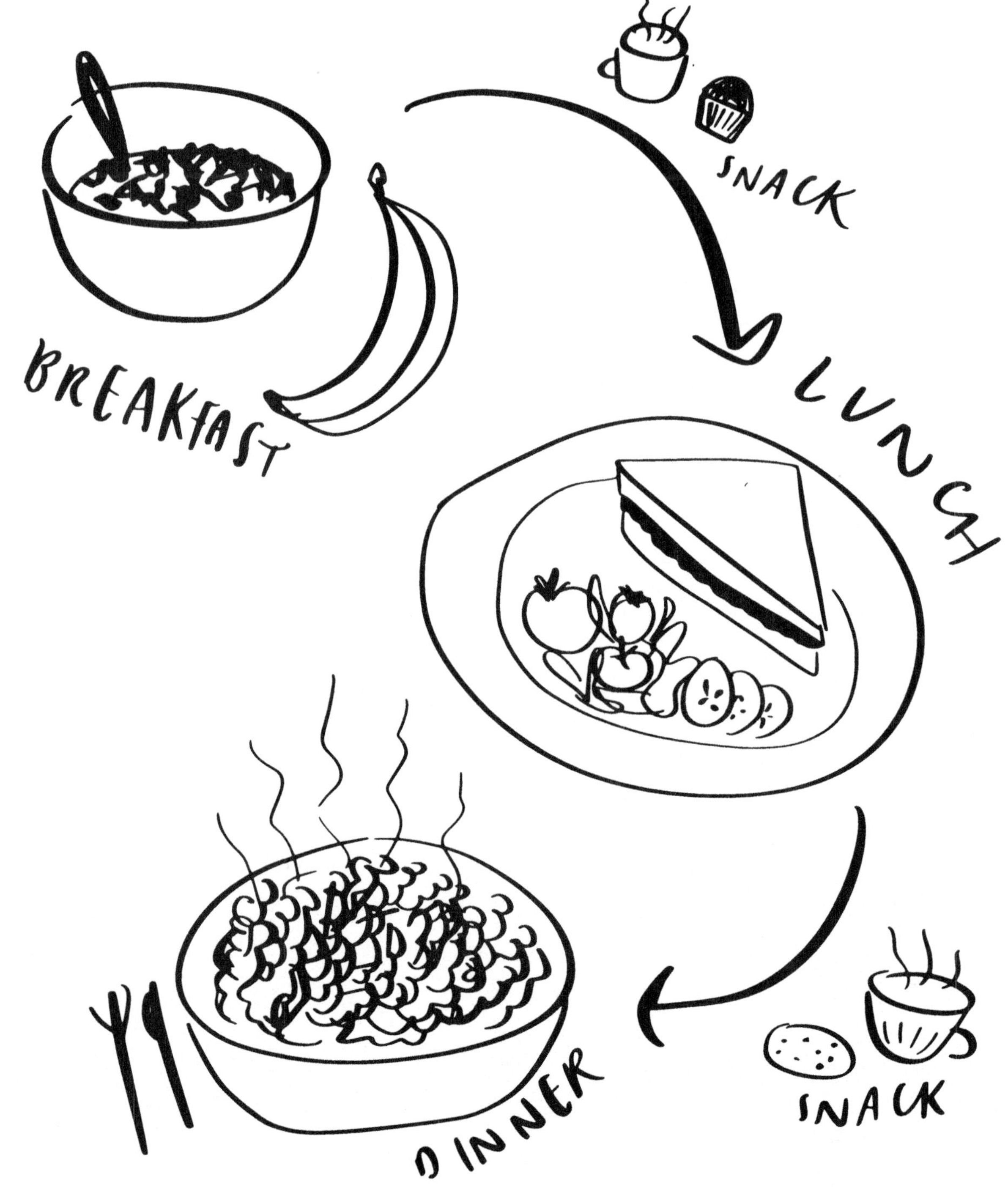
SNACK
BREAKFAST
LUNCH
SNACK
DINNER

DAILY BREAD

GOD SPEAKS & FEEDS US AS WE READ HIS WORDS

"Man does not live on bread alone, but on every word that comes from the mouth of the Lord."
Deuteronomy 8:3

Some people say that God never speaks to them, but if you ask them when they last read their Bible, they can't remember.

"I'm hungry!"

"When did you last eat?"

"I haven't eaten today, or actually for days, I forgot."

"Well, go and eat!"

The main way that God speaks is through the Bible and that's why it's important that we read it regularly and consistently. This will allow the Holy Spirit the opportunity to make something leap out to us and become alive in our hearts. Just in the same way that I need to eat daily or else I feel weak, I find that when I read the Bible every day it gives me the strength that I need for the day.

The Bible is God's written word to us. He's shared it with us so that He can speak to us through it. But the Bible isn't just for information. It's also for bringing about our transformation, which happens as the Holy Spirit uses God's words to change us to be more like Christ.

Whenever reading the Bible, it's always good to ask the Holy Spirit to speak to us through it. The more we know and memorise Scripture, the more we'll establish a library-like resource within our memory and heart that the Holy Spirit can use to speak to us, both for our own good and for the blessing of others. If we want to be people who share God's words with others, we must know God's Word for ourself.[1]

IDEA – DO

Decide to read a bit of the Bible every day.

1 The Bible Project video series have helped me *enormously* with my knowledge and understanding of Scripture. I highly recommend them. They can be accessed free on YouTube and they also have a Bible-in-a year app which is excellent.

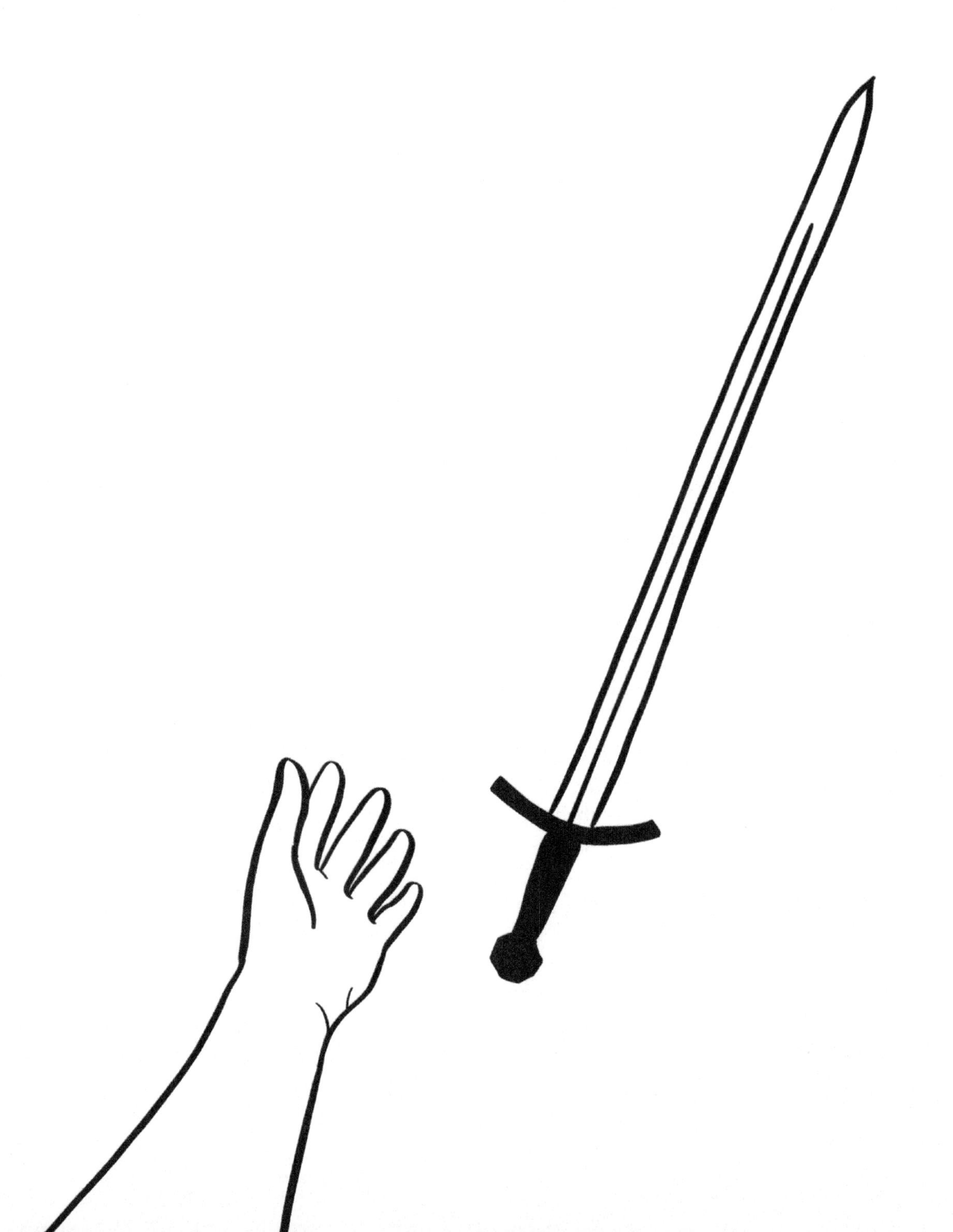

THE SWORD

SCRIPTURE ARMS & PROTECTS US

"The sword of the Spirit, which is the word of God."
Ephesians 6:17

A few years ago I was doing a lot of reading and, in my defence, they were all 'good Christian books' full of Bible quotes! I was also reading my Bible, but more like 'snacking' on it, rather than 'feasting'. I tried to convince myself that the combination of good Christian books along with my Bible 'snacking' was giving me a sufficiently 'balanced diet'. However, deep down I knew that this wasn't the case. God wanted me to engage with His Word in a wholehearted, committed way. But I procrastinated. *"Tomorrow, tomorrow!"* But tomorrow never comes and I was enjoying my 'good Christian books', so I ignored the Holy Spirit's quiet but persistent voice.

But then God decided it was time to intervene. I was at a conference and had gone forward to get prayed for something. A man I did not know came over to me and shared what He felt God was saying. "God says, *"You've dropped your sword and you need to pick it back up again!"* "

As soon as he'd said that, I remembered Ephesians 6:17 *"The sword of the Spirit, which is the word of God."*[1] In that moment I felt my loving Father rebuke me tenderly, *"Anna, now is the time. Take hold of My Word."*

God is so gracious and kind because along with those words He also gave me a renewed passion for Scripture. From that day on, I've grown more and more in love with God's written word, and more importantly, the Author of the words. I now look forward to reading and feasting on God's bread every morning.[2]

IDEA – REFLECT

Have you dropped your 'sword'?

1 I like this quote - *"Not reading the Bible is like riding into battle with a banana instead of a broad sword."* Dan Gould

2 *"Visit many good books but live in the Bible"* C. H. Spurgeon

a promise

GOD'S PROVISION AND PROTECTION

THE BABY STORY

GOD SPEAKS THROUGH SCRIPTURE

"Does he speak and then not act Does he promise and not fulfill?"

Numbers 23:19

I had just been diagnosed with having a brain tumour.[1] The doctors had discovered it following an MRI brain scan that had been requested in order to find out why we were struggling to have children. The effect of the tumour was to make my body think it was pregnant when it wasn't, and since you can't get pregnant whilst you're already pregnant, my body was in a state of barrenness. The consultant explained that he could put me on some powerful medication, but if I was to become pregnant I'd then need to come off it immediately. I was warned that my chances of miscarrying would be above average.

I remember sitting down to read my Bible one morning whilst trying to process all of this information. At the time I was going through the book of Exodus and that day came to Chapter 23. As I read my passages for the day, this verse leapt out at me: *"...none will miscarry or be barren in your land."*[2]

In that moment, I felt that the Holy Spirit was bringing it alive to me in a personal way and was saying *"this will be true of you too".* It gave me faith and hope to believe that we would indeed conceive a child. And we did! A few months later I found out I was pregnant. Two years after that, I had another child. I have never had a miscarriage.

In God's great grace and mercy, He protected and provided for us. And it came out of a promise that was spoken as I read God's written word.

IDEA – REFLECT

Are there any promises you're still waiting for?

Keep praying!

1 It's called a microprolactinoma and is not life-threatening, so please don't be concerned.

2 Exodus 23:26

another promise

GOD SAID HE WOULD BUILD US A HOUSE

THE HOUSE STORY

GOD IS TRUE TO HIS WORD

"So is my word that goes out from my mouth: It will not return to me empty, but will accomplish what I desire and achieve the purpose for which I sent it."
Isaiah 55:11

A few years ago, my husband and I were in our kitchen talking about whether we should move. We had two fast-growing boys and no room to host guests so we really felt like we needed some extra space. I remember saying to Daniel how I was really struggling to know how to pray. The Bible says we should be content in all circumstances and yet we had this desire for a bigger house. I felt that I didn't know what God's will was and I was struggling.[1]

I prayed *"Father, we want a bigger house so we can host lots of people. Yet, we don't know if this is just our own heart's desire, or if this is from you. Help us to know Your will so we can pray in line with it".*

Then I began my daily Bible reading. At the time, I was going through the book of Chronicles and that morning, one of the verses seemed to come to life as I read it. *"I declare to you that the Lord will build a house for you".*[2]

Just minutes before we'd been asking God about what His will was and five minutes later I read this. I felt like God was giving us His answer!

And God did just as He said He would. A couple of years later, we moved into a brand new house that didn't actually exist at the time I read those words. It was also a house that we couldn't afford, but God provided every penny – with the promise came the provision.

IDEA – READ

Deuteronomy 7:9

"Know therefore that the Lord your God is God; he is the faithful God"

1 1 John 5:14 says, *"This is the confidence we have in approaching God: that if we ask anything according to his will, he hears us. And if we know that he hears us—whatever we ask—we know that we have what we asked of him."*

2 1 Chronicles 17:10

ASK FOR BIG, BOLD, AUDACIOUS, OUTRAGEOUS, SPECIFIC THINGS

VERSE OF THE YEAR

GOD'S FOCUS HELPS DIRECT US

"Then he said, "Take the arrows," and the king took them. Elisha told him, "Strike the ground." He struck it three times and stopped. The man of God was angry with him and said, "You should have struck the ground five or six times."
2 Kings 13:18–19

A wise spiritual mother of mine told me about a practice she does at the beginning of every year which is to ask God for a Bible verse for that year. I've been doing this for several years now and have found it extremely helpful. For 2020, the story of 2 Kings 13:18–19 came into my head.

Elisha the Prophet asks the King of Israel to strike the ground with the arrow (which represented victory). The King does this, but only strikes it three times. Elisha gets angry because the King didn't boldly seize the moment and strike the ground more times! He settled for less than God was willing to give him.

I felt God say, *"You don't expect much from me! Why are you settling for less when you could have more?"* I don't think when I meet God He's going to say to me, *"Anna, your expectations of me were too high..."* I don't think He'll say that to anyone!

Having this Bible verse has completely changed the way that I pray. I now feel challenged by God to pray big, outrageous and audacious prayers. To expect more and ask for more because He is the God of the impossible.[1]

IDEA – DO

Ask God to lead you to a Bible verse that He wants you to focus on this year.

1 *"Is anything too hard for the Lord?"* Genesis 18:14

DETAILS
GOOD NEWS!
GOD'S
WORDS
TRUTH
THIS WAY?
OR THIS WAY?
N
W
E
S

SIX REASONS

WHY GOD'S WRITTEN WORD IS PRECIOUS

"Jesus answered, "It is written..."
Matthew 4:4

There are many reasons to love God's written Word, here are six.

1. The *authority* of the Bible.
The last word always goes to the inspired word of God; it is final. (No person can claim the same authority for their words as for the Bible).

2. The *sufficiency* of the Bible.
It is complete and contains all we need to know about God, salvation and godly living. God's word is *enough.* (We are told not to add to the words of the Bible, no more words are needed).[1]

3. The *inerrancy* and *truthfulness* of the Bible.
It is without error and contains no lies, half-truths or blind alleys. (No person can claim all their words are without any errors. Some false prophets try to deceive).

4. The *clarity* of the Bible.
It can be understood. The saving message of Jesus is taught plainly in Scripture and doesn't require external official teaching to tell us what it means. Though it is not simple, it can be known. (In contrast, when we prophesy *"we know in part and we prophesy in part").*[2]

5. The *necessity* of the Bible.
We need God's word to tell us how to be saved, how to live and who Christ is. General revelation is not enough to save us. God's written word is *necessary.*[3]

6. The final reason to love Scripture is because *Jesus* does. Jesus regularly, repeatedly quoted from Scripture throughout His ministry.

IDEA – REFLECT

Which of these points is most important to you?

1 *"Do not add to what I command you and do not subtract from it."* Deuteronomy 4:2

2 1 Corinthians 13:9

3 For further detail on this I recommend reading Kevin DeYoung's book, *"Taking God at His Word".*

HOW GOD SPEAKS

THE WIDE VARIETY OF CREATIVE WAYS GOD CAN CONNECT TO US.

We've thought about the fact that God loves to talk to us, His children (aka. His sheep), and that we need to learn how to still our hearts in order to listen (and 'look') for His voice. We've also discussed the importance of being rooted in the Bible and the fact that God has already spoken to us through it.

Let's now talk a bit more about the personal and creative ways we can *see, hear* or even *feel* the voice of God in our everyday lives (also known as "Revelation"). This can be through our *internal* and *external* world.

you know me

INNERMOST DETAIL

GOD KNOWS EVERYTHING ABOUT YOU

Psalm 139 is a wonderful piece of poetry describing the level and detail to which God knows us. Let's read some of it together.

You have searched me, Lord,
and you know me.
You know when I sit and when I rise;
you perceive my thoughts from afar.
You discern my going out
and my lying down;
you are familiar with all my ways.
Before a word is on my tongue
you, Lord, know it completely.
You hem me in behind and before,
and you lay your hand upon me.
Such knowledge is too wonderful for me,
too lofty for me to attain.
Where can I go from your Spirit?
Where can I flee from your presence?
If I go up to the heavens, you are there;
if I make my bed in the depths,
you are there.
If I rise on the wings of the dawn,
if I settle on the far side of the sea,
even there your hand will guide me,
your right hand will hold me fast.
If I say, "Surely the darkness will hide me
and the light become night around me,"
even the darkness will not be dark to you;
the night will shine like the day,
for darkness is as light to you.
For you created my inmost being;
you knit me together
in my mother's womb.
I praise you because I am fearfully
and wonderfully made;
your works are wonderful,
I know that full well.
My frame was not hidden from you
when I was made in the secret place,
when I was woven together
in the depths of the earth.
Your eyes saw my unformed body;
all the days ordained for me
were written in your book
before one of them came to be.
How precious to me are
your thoughts, God![1]
How vast is the sum of them!

IDEA – REFLECT

Which of these verses stands out to you the most?

1 I love that Our God is a thinking God who is willing to share His thoughts with us, His children!

God Spoke...

THE CREATOR

GOD CAN CONNECT IN CREATIVE WAYS

"God said... and there was"
Genesis 1:3

The first verse in the first chapter of the first book of the Bible says, *"In the beginning God created the heavens and the earth"* (Genesis 1:1).

"God said..." and God created. I love that.

God's words are powerful. They bring life, light, creativity, order, structure, direction and hope.

God is The Creator, He is creative, that's part of His nature, He loves variety. This is relevant because it not only means we get to admire His creativity from the big toucan's bill to the aurora borealis,[1] but also because we should expect to see His creativity in the way that He speaks to us.

Our Creator Father who knows *"every hair on your head"*[2] can, in any given moment, use any of the things He knows about you to communicate to you. He could remind you of one of your *memories* because it's relevant to your current situation or He could put a *song lyric* in your head because there's a line in it that He wants to talk to you about. God can use any of your unique experiences or qualities to connect with you.

The reason it's important that we know this is that otherwise we may dismiss what He's saying because we don't think God talks that way, or that it's somehow 'not spiritual enough' to be God. But to God, everything is spiritual, because He created everything.

IDEA – THINK

How might God have spoken to you in creative ways before?

1 Apparently the best place to see this is in Fairbanks, Alaska.

2 It's true! See Luke 12:7. He also knows all the movies you've watched, all the podcasts you've listened to, all the adverts you've seen and all the comments you've ever written and read on the internet. There's literally nothing that He doesn't know about you!

HOW DOES GOD SPEAK TO ME? SEARCH

A PROCESS

YOUR PERSONAL JOURNEY

God values friendship and wants a relationship with you that is personal. God may therefore interact with you in a way that will be unique and different to others, because God treats everyone individually.

I love to research.[1] God knows that about me because He created me to be like that. Part of what I've discovered on my walk with God is that He will often put something on my heart and then encourage me to research the subject.[2] As I research and ask God to speak to me in what I'm doing, I find that He makes the relevant things stand out somehow.

This has been part of my individual journey. For you it might be different because you may hate researching things, but God knows that too! The way God speaks to you will be different to the way He speaks to me.

I love it when people start to realise this truth. After one afternoon of seminar teaching, a woman shared the following with me.

"I didn't think I could hear God's voice. Now I think that maybe God is speaking to me after all, I just didn't realise it! The story of Snow White kept on coming into my mind and how she was asleep in a glass coffin and her prince had to come and wake her up. I think maybe Jesus is saying that we, the church, are asleep and that He's coming back soon so we need to wake up!"

You'll need to work out how God speaks to you *personally*. This may take time and involve a *process* of trial and error. Try to enjoy the journey – it's just as important as the destination because it's all about an ongoing, growing relationship.

IDEA – REFLECT

What are you discovering on your journey with God?

1 I spent ten years of my life researching Huntington's disease. But I love researching just about anything...

2 Often involving Google (sometimes even Wikipedia!) - how 'unspiritual' does that seem?! ...

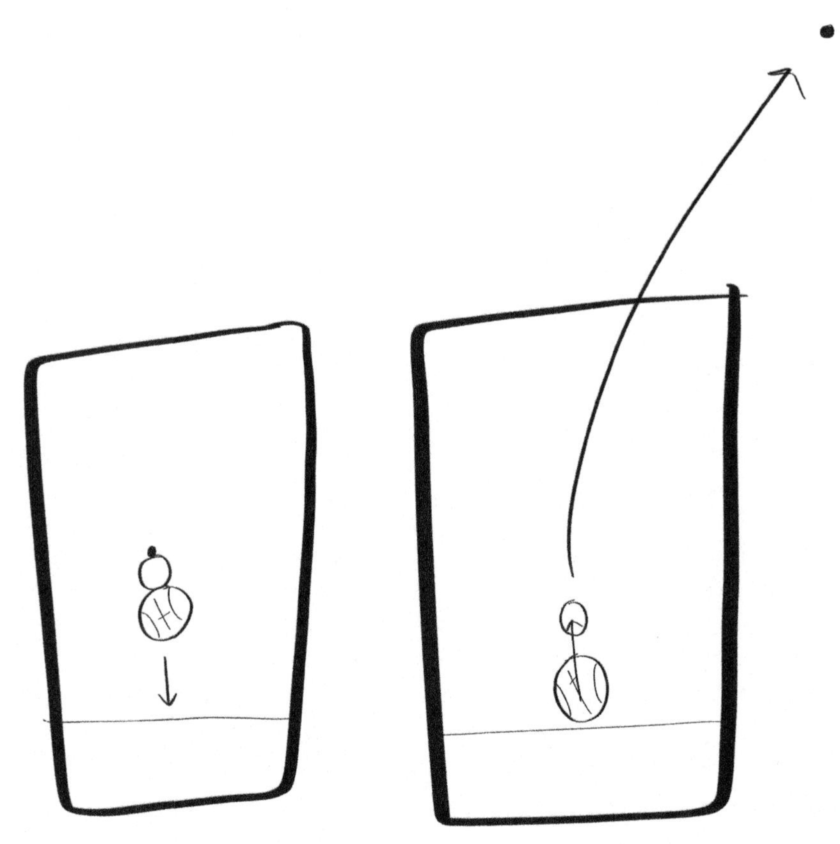

OUR OWN LANGUAGE

GOD SPEAKS IN WAYS WE UNDERSTAND

In Scripture, we see how Jesus used parables about fishing to speak to fishermen, sheep to communicate with shepherds and seeds to connect to farmers. He knew how to talk in a way that others would understand.

So, if you love sports, God will probably use sports analogies to speak to you, or sewing, sketching or surfing, depending on what you're into. God knows what 'languages' you speak.

My background is in science. It's one of the 'languages' God knows I speak. Once I was learning about a particular physics experiment - the 'Stacked Ball Drop.' The experiment involves placing a small golf ball on top of a bouncy ball on top of a basket ball and then dropping the whole stack. What happens is that the golf ball is propelled 800% of its dropped height.[1]

I felt God use this as a visual illustration of what I was going to see happen in my lifetime. He was going to move on earth in a powerful and unprecedented way.[2] And this was going to be the result of the prayers of His people.

Science is one of my languages, but for you it may be something different. God speaks to us in a way that is unique to us as individuals.

When I was living at home, I had an arrangement with my parents. If we were ever in a situation in which we didn't feel safe, but didn't feel like we could communicate that, we would ring them up and say, *"I need my asthma inhaler."* That was code for, *"come and get me!"* None of my family have asthma, we don't own any inhalers. No-one else knew what that sentence really meant.

God knows how to talk to you.

IDEA – REFLECT

Hearing God's voice is a bit like the game Charades. It works best when you're familiar with the way the other person thinks.

1 Physics Girl on YouTube can demonstrate and explain this well to you.

2 This verse seemed relevant, *"Before all your people I will do wonders never before done in any nation in all the world. The people you live among will see how awesome is the work that I, the Lord, will do for you."* Exodus 34:10

THOUGHTS & IMAGINATION

GOD CREATED YOUR BRAIN & CAN USE IT

"You perceive my thoughts from afar"
Psalm 139:2

God can speak through your mind in different ways. For example, spontaneous thoughts, words or pictures (static or moving) and your imagination.[1] My son describes it like a puppet show going on in his head!

Once when I was praying, I found myself seeing (in my mind) waves on the sea shore. Instead of rolling forwards, the waves were rolling backwards. Then a spontaneous sentence came into my thoughts, *"the tide is turning".* I didn't understand what God meant, so I asked Him. A memory then came into my head.

Six of us had gone out crabbing and after an hour or so, and a lot of effort, we'd only caught two old crabs. We thought we must've had the wrong technique, the wrong bait or the wrong something else! Not entirely defeated, we returned at high tide. This time within five minutes even our youngest was pulling out buckets so full of crabs they were falling out! Apparently crabbing is best at high tide. When the time was right, it was just so easy. It was nothing to do with clever technique, we were just there, ready, waiting and willing to give it a go.

In my heart I felt a quiet voice say, *"the tide is turning, high tide is coming and the 'catch' will be so great that even the littlest children will be hauling in 'buckets.' Are you ready and willing?"*[2]

I felt God was sharing this so we as a church could be prepared to share the Gospel effectively and disciple many new believers. And that meant equipping even our very youngest members.

IDEA – PRAY

"Father, please bless my mind, imagination and thoughts."

1 Some people think the imagination is bad. But just like the rest of your body, when we give it to God and ask Him to bless it He can use it in a powerful way.

2 *"The days are coming," declares the Lord, "when the reaper will be overtaken by the plowman"* Amos 9:13

MEMORIES

GOD CAN USE YOUR PAST TO SPEAK TO YOU

The first medically verifiable healing that I ever witnessed was a boy called Rex.[1]

It started with a memory. I'd once gone grocery shopping and my trolley had a wheel that didn't quite reach the ground so it kept spinning around.[2] This memory kept coming back to me for no apparent reason, so I wondered whether it might be God. I asked him about it and felt God was saying that someone had an issue of asymmetry in their body that He wanted heal.

I shared this one Sunday and at the end of the service a mother approached me. She described how one of her son's legs was longer than the other and was also bent. When he sat with his legs stretched out in front of him, the back of his knee couldn't touch the floor (a bit like the trolley wheel I'd described). Rex was therefore potentially going to have to have his leg in a thigh high plaster cast for several months in order to correct this issue.

We prayed twice, on two separate Sundays. On both occasions, he felt nothing and we saw nothing. But we knew something had happened and that God always hears our prayers.[3]

After the consultant met with little Rex he was left perplexed. He said that even though he'd measured both legs and taken x-rays, he 'must have somehow made a mistake, because both legs were perfectly straight and exactly the same length'. He had expected to treat Rex, but no longer needed to. And Rex was discharged from hospital.

God had healed Rex!

IDEA – REFLECT

Has God ever spoken to you using a memory?

---

1 I've changed his name. I think Rex is a cool name even though it's often used as a dog's name!

2 It was very annoying.

3 I used to think that prayer was like trying to fly a paper aeroplane through a letter box - sometimes you got it through the small gap, other times you missed. But this isn't true. Every prayer that is prayed is heard by God. Nothing misses His ears.

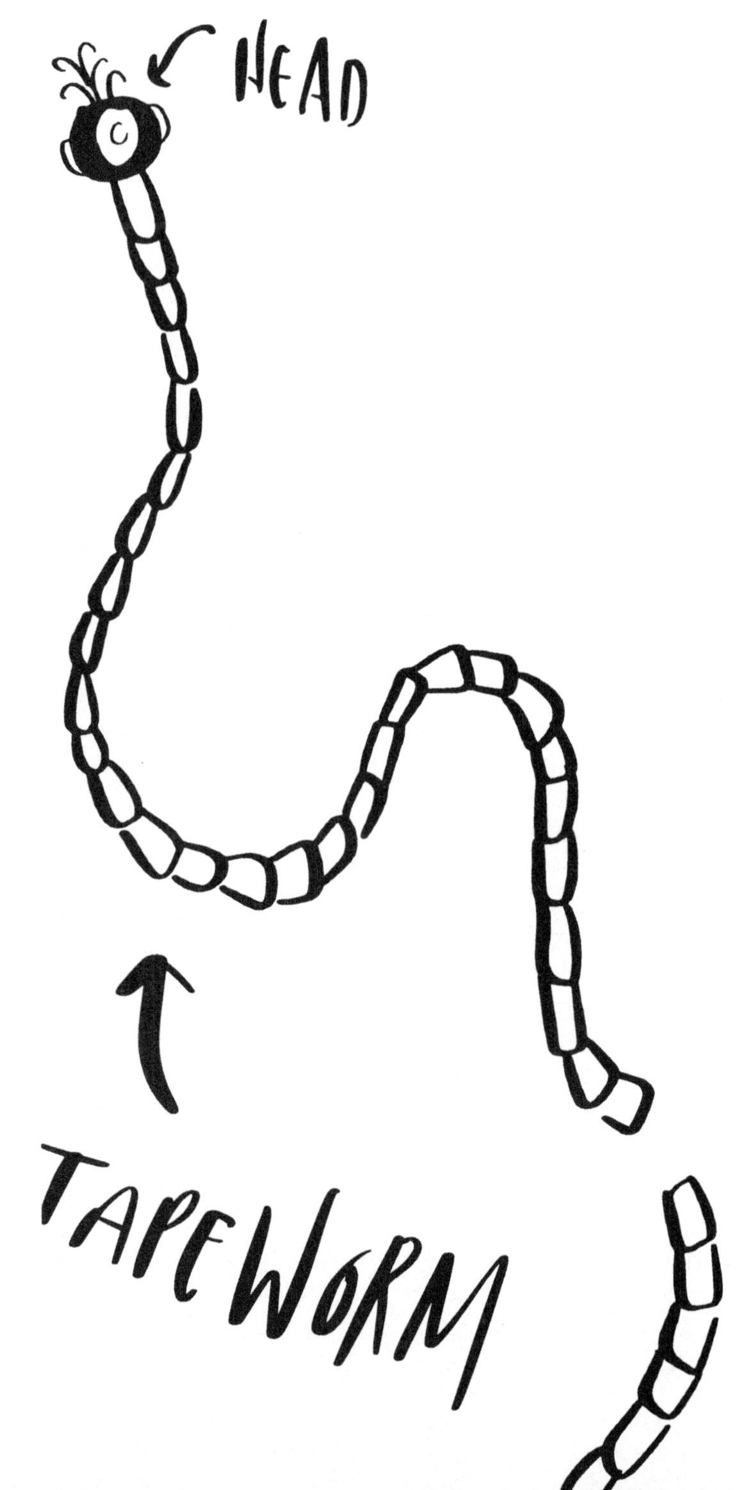
HEAD
TAPEWORM

KNOWLEDGE

GOD CAN USE FACTS YOU KNOW

"You have searched me, Lord, and you know me."
Psalm 139:1

God knows everything you've ever learnt, all those random animal facts that you once knew as a child, all the bits of cereal box trivia you've collected over the years and every lesson you were taught at school, even the really boring ones. And He can use any of that information to communicate something to you.

I remember once praying for someone and as I did so, a picture of a tapeworm came into my mind. Growing up abroad meant that I was familiar with some of the different parasites that exist (one of the reasons why we had to boil our milk and not drink tap water when we lived in Nepal).

The tapeworm is quite alien-like to look at, but it's also cleverly designed for survival. It consists of one main head surrounded with multiple hooks. These hooks latch onto the host organism enabling it to feed off the host, robbing it of its nutrition. Attached to the head is the body which is made up of many segments. These segments are designed to shed. If you managed to get hold of the end of the worm and pulled, a segment would come off but the head would remain undisturbed. Ultimately, when treating someone with tapeworm, you need to focus on getting to the head in order to remove it.

As I was praying with and talking to this person, I could see that we were actually dealing with many different 'segments' of issues, but that they weren't the heart of the matter. I knew we needed to get to the heart of the matter because it was there that she needed freedom the most. In this particular case, it transpired that anger was at the head of it all and so this is where we focused our prayers.

IDEA – REFLECT

God has solutions to your problems.

Ask Him for help and He'll show you the way.

THE FIRST THING TO DO IS PRAY

Z

Z Z Z

Z Z Z

DREAMS

GOD CAN SPEAK AS WE SLEEP

"Your young men will see visions, your old men will dream dreams"
Acts 2:17

Sometimes God gets our attention or speaks to us through night-time dreams.

Once whilst I was on holiday in Sinai, Egypt, I had a dream in which my eldest brother was on a motorbike in the dry, winding hills of some foreign land. In my dream, he was riding fast along one of the dusty, narrow tracks but didn't turn one of the corners sharply enough and so rode right over the edge. I remember feeling horrified as I saw him in mid-air, just like the roadrunner and coyote cartoon. Even though he was suspended but alive in front of me, I knew he was about to plummet to his death.

I woke up sweating and sobbing, deeply disturbed by this dream,so I started to pray for his protection and sent him a text message to make sure that he was OK.

The next day I found out that while I had been in bed in Egypt praying for him, he had been in a club in the UK and had got involved in an awful fight which, let's just say, involved a plank of wood with a nail stuck in the back of it.

I really do believe that God gave me that dream in order to get me to pray into what could have been a very harmful situation.[1]

When God gets our attention, the first thing to do is pray.

IDEA - DO

Start to record your dreams.

Ask God to speak through them.

1 Personally, I don't believe you need a Christian dream interpretation book in order to interpret dreams from God - Joseph and Daniel didn't have one! Genesis 40:8 says *"Do not interpretations belong to God?"* If God gave a revelation to you in a dream then He will also give you the interpretation if you ask for it.

NATURAL SENSES

GOD CAN USE YOUR BODY TO COMMUNICATE TO YOU

"Offer your bodies as a living sacrifice, holy and pleasing to God-this is your true and proper worship."
Romans 12:1

Since God created you, He can use any part of you to communicate or get your attention. This includes all of your five senses.[1]

I remember reading a story about a man who suddenly smelt fresh oranges. Since there were no oranges around, he thought God might be trying to speak. He felt God say that the pastor's son in the church to which he was travelling was very sick, but the doctors didn't know why. But God knew why - it was due to a serious Vitamin C deficiency. The man shared this information with the pastor and, as a result, his son was healed.[2]

Here's a different story. A friend of mine has *synaesthesia*, a neurological condition that causes the brain to process information in the form of several senses at once. For example, he sometimes hears words and numbers and at the same time consistently sees a certain colour or texture.[3]

He once told me how the number 40 came into his mind when he met me. To him, 40 is a dark blue colour. There were other things that he associated with the same colour (such as the book of Deuteronomy). As he pieced these things together, he felt that God was possibly saying something. When he shared it with me he was spot on! And I was really blessed.

God can speak through our senses.

IDEA - PRAY

"Father God, please bless my body and speak through it."

---

1 E.g. He could give you a pain sensation in your body to let you know He wanted to heal someone with a problem in that area.

2 Hirtler, R. (2014) Balancing the prophetic. Equipping the Church in the Prophetic Ministry. Page 38.

3 However nobody else would associate the same words or numbers because there's actually no logical connection.

EMOTIONS

GOD CAN SHARE HIS FEELINGS WITH US

"Moved with compassion, Jesus touched their eyes, and at once they received their sight"
Matthew 20:34 (BSB)

Sometimes my boys will put their heads on my stomach and then I'll laugh. For some reason feeling me laughing in this way sends them off into fits of hysterics. My laughter triggers off their laughter simply because their head is touching my body. This kind of mirroring of emotion can also happen when you are consoling someone who is crying deeply; their sobbing body can make you start to cry as well.

We often read in the Gospels about how, *"moved with compassion, Jesus..."* [did something].[1] As we spend time with our Heavenly Father, we may find that we start to recognise His emotions. His emotions can become our emotions.[2] God may lead you to a person by sharing His heart with you (for example, compassion or sadness). If this happens, ask God what to do next.

Peace is another way of recognising God's heart. As we grow in being sensitive to the peace of the Holy Spirit, we can become aware of when it increases or decreases as we go places and meet people. Sometimes we may notice a peace when looking at a person or when we're with them and it can mean that God is trying to get your attention because He wants to say something.

IDEA – REFLECT

Recognising God's heart will get easier the more time you spend with Him.

1 The Greek verb word for *"to feel compassion"* is *"Splagchnizomai"* which means to have the experience of such emotion that you feel it in your stomach, liver and intestines!

2 I want to add something which is hopefully obvious. Sometimes, although our emotions, hormones, dreams etc. may feel very 'spiritual' in the moment, it's *not* always God trying to speak! That's why we need to ask the Holy Spirit for *discernment* to help us tell the difference. This is also a good reason to *wait a while* before rushing ahead with anything that we think is from God. Sometimes as we wait we realise it wasn't God after all, we just needed to eat some chocolate and calm down (or is that just me?!)

WHAT DO
YOU SEE?

SURROUNDINGS

GOD CAN SPEAK THROUGH THE WORLD AROUND US

"'What do you see, Jeremiah?' 'I see the branch of an almond tree'"
Jeremiah 1:11

In this passage, God was teaching Jeremiah how to interpret and understand what God was showing him and that God could use objects and natural surroundings to speak.

We were out one leafy, golden afternoon and noticed a frantic movement in the fence nearby - a trapped squirrel. He had obviously misjudged the size of the gap in the fence and had got stuck.

It was painful to watch this wide-eyed creature struggling so hard to free himself. We knew his best efforts were simply in vain and if we left him, he would die. In the end, we got some wire cutters and cut the frightened redhead loose. Immediately he darted off to celebrate his new found freedom in the fading light.

I later felt God use this to remind me of what He'd done in my life. Before we ask Jesus into our lives we are trapped by our sin. Scripture tells us that the consequence of sin is death.[1] No matter how much we strive and struggle, we cannot fix our situation. We need Jesus. When we invite Jesus into our lives He rescues us from the fate we deserve and frees us from sin and death.[2]

That day I thanked Jesus again for the gift of life and hope that He gave me, through His death and resurrection.

IDEA – REFLECT

As we walk God can talk, if we have eyes to see and ears to hear.

Be expectant!

1 *"For the wages of sin is death, but the gift of God is eternal life in Christ Jesus our Lord."* Romans 6:23.

2 *"It is for freedom that Christ has set us free."* Galatians 5:1 *"The Spirit who gives life has set you free from the law of sin and death."* Romans 8:2

M T W T F S S

SYMBOLS OR SIGNS

GOD CAN GET OUR ATTENTION IN DIFFERENT WAYS

Sometimes God might speak to you through signs, colours, numbers, etc. in your surroundings.

At one point in my life I felt a bit lost and really wanted to know what God's agenda was for my life. What should I focus on and what were distractions? I needed God's perspective.

Then a strange thing started to happen. I began to see the number 1818 around a lot.

After puzzling over this, I remembered reading a book in which the author[1] also described seeing a certain set of numbers frequently. He then felt God directed Him to a Bible passage using the numbers as chapter and verse references. This was happening to me as well! God spoke to me in a very meaningful way through chapter 18, verse 18 of a particular book in the Bible. Almost immediately after this, the same thing happened with the numbers 0808. Again I felt led to a particular Bible verse.

Significantly for me, the verses connected to 18:18 and 08:08 mentioned the two things that had previously been spoken to me about God's heart for my life. It was therefore a wonderful reminder and confirmation. What made it even more special is that my birthday is the 18th of August[2] or 18.08. I felt God was pointing out that even my birthdate was no accident!

At this point, I feel I need to emphasise the need to continually ask God for His wisdom and discernment. God's not going to be speaking through every colour, symbol and number that you will ever see so please don't start reading into everything. Remember we're talking about walking in relationship and not about deciphering a code and relying on a formula.

IDEA – PRAY

"Holy Spirit, please make it clear when You are and aren't speaking!"

---

1 Sheets, D. (1996) Intercessory Prayer. California: Regal.

2 Now you know my birthday you can send me a card. No one seems to send cards these days, it's very sad.

£TUNA

I DISMISSED IT

CONNECTIONS

GOD CAN SPEAK TO & THROUGH OUR RELATIONSHIPS

"Walk with the wise and become wise"

Proverbs 13:12

In January 2019, I remember reading about a Japanese sushi tycoon who'd just paid a fat £2.5 million for a giant tuna fish, making it the most expensive in the world. Two things happened as I read that article. The first was that I was in total shock that anyone would pay that amount of money for a fish[1] but, second, it felt as though the Holy Spirit was giving 'weight' to the article somehow, as though He was saying, *"I have something to say about this!"*

As I paused to give space to what God might be wanting to say, the phrase, *"I'm going to bring a precious Tuna into your life"* popped unexpectedly into my head. Probably a bit like you, I hadn't the faintest idea what on earth that meant, so quickly dismissed it as irrelevant.

But was it?

That same month, I noticed that my eldest son was becoming close friends with a wonderful, kind-hearted boy from Turkey.[2] Seeing the deep friendship and brother-like bond that was naturally developing between them, I decided to invite him over for a playdate one day.

Through this connection, I've now got to know his mother. To this day she is one of my closest and dearest friends. She is a devout muslim and has taught me so much about her faith, country and culture. I have been incredibly impacted by her. Another thing I've got to know is her surname.

It's *"Tuna".*

God told me He was going to bring a *"precious Tuna"* into my life and He did.

IDEA - PRAY

"Father, please connect me with people you want me to know."

1 I mean, it's just a fish. (The full story can be found here: https://www.bbc.co.uk/news/world-asia-46767370)

2 I've found that God often uses my children to connect me to people He wants me to get to know.

THAT'S
JUST
ODD

EVERYDAY EXPERIENCES

GOD CAN SPEAK THROUGH THINGS THAT HAPPEN

"God called to him from within the bush, 'Moses! Moses!'"
Exodus 3:4

Exodus 3 recounts the story of when the angel of the Lord appeared to Moses in flames of fire from within a bush. The bush was on fire but did not burn up. So Moses went over to investigate. Then God spoke.

God can speak through *ordinary* and *unusual* experiences that make you think, *"how odd!"*

"Your taxi is here!" a taxi driver announced at my door. I paused, confused. I hadn't ordered a taxi. I politely told him he had the wrong address. Now he became confused. He referred back to his iPad and asked, *"Are you sure?"* He showed me the order and there was my address. Strange. I'd no idea what had happened, but reassured him that I'd not ordered it.

45 minutes later, my door bell rang again. A different taxi driver. Exactly the same experience. Again I replied, *"I didn't order it. You've got the wrong address."*

Later that day I was praying for a friend who was trying to move house. I asked God if there was anything He wanted to say to her because I knew that moving house was a difficult time. Almost immediately I sensed a quiet reply, *"You heard my words today."* I reflected back on the day, my unusual encounter and the words I'd spoken, *"I didn't order it. You've got the wrong address."*

I wrote to my friend and described what had happened and that possibly God was saying, *"twice you'll think you've found the right place but actually you've got the wrong address!"*

My friend replied saying exactly that - twice they'd thought they'd found the right place to move into and twice it had fallen through. This had been very confusing for them as a family. God knew this and wanted to reassure them that He had a plan.

IDEA – REFLECT

Has anything odd happened to you recently?

Could God be trying to speak?

STOP

A SINGLE WORD OR WORDS

GOD CAN PUT A WORD OR SENTENCE IN YOUR MIND

"Ephphatha!"[1]

Mark 7:34

God does not waste His words, every word God speaks is meaningful. That's why we need to pay careful attention if we think He's spoken.

One weekend I'd been shopping and had parked my car next to a recreation ground. At the time that I was leaving I was vaguely aware that a few boys were playing football nearby. Just as I was about to reverse my car out of my bay, I heard a loud voice in my head.

"STOP!"

I stopped, somewhat shocked. What was that about?

Then I saw a little boy come out from underneath my car. One of the kids had kicked the football into the parking bays and it had rolled right where I was parked. The boy had rushed to retrieve the ball and was on his hands and knees under my car just as I was about to reverse out. When my engine started he was not visible in my mirrors and was paralysed with fear about what to do.

But God knew he was there.

IDEA – THINK

Learning to be quick to listen and obey is an important part of responding to God's voice.

1 This means *"Be opened!"* Jesus spoke these words to a man who was deaf and could hardly talk and as a result he was healed.

VOLUME

VOLUME

GOD CAN CHOOSE HOW LOUDLY HE SPEAKS

"After the wind there was an earthquake, but the Lord was not in the earthquake. After the earthquake came a fire, but the Lord was not in the fire. And after the fire came a gentle whisper."
1 Kings 19:11-12

In addition to speaking in many *different ways,* God can also choose His *volume.* In the example of the boy under my car, I felt the voice was *loud* but still in my head. God can also speak loudly as an *audible voice* that others can hear, for example when God the Father spoke to Jesus when He was baptised (Matthew 17:5). However, most of the time I think God chooses to speak *quietly,* as a *whisper.*[1]

Sometimes that whisper can be so soft that it comes across as a *persistent urge.*

In our neighbourhood, after Christmas we get inundated with charity bags asking to be filled with good quality items. One January, I'd done my best to fill as many bags as possible. Amongst our donations were quite a lot of books. Before putting them in the bags, I'd checked inside them all to make sure I hadn't left any personal bookmarks or notes. They were all fine, so I was confident to give them away.

However, the day before we were due to give the bags away, I started to feel a persistent urge to check the bags again. The urge became such a relentless hum in my ear, that I decided to check them again. When I came to the final page of the final book, I saw what the urge was about. Written there in my small, clear handwriting were all my bank details written for safe keeping. I can't actually remember writing them, but God did and He was protecting me.

IDEA - THINK

Do you expect God's voice to be loud?

Often it's a whisper.

1 Most of the stories that I have shared with you in this chapter came to me as a soft, quiet voice and this is why we spoke earlier about the need for silencing the 'chatter' in our lives.

CONVERSATION

UNDERSTAND WHAT GOD IS SAYING

In the previous chapter we talked about the many, varied, creative ways that God can connect His heart and thoughts to ours (sometimes referred to as *Revelation*). But let's backtrack a bit now and talk more about three things:

1. How God sometimes gets our *attention* in the first place so that we can become aware that he wants to begin a conversation.

2. How to get to the *heart* of what God is saying and not miss the main point (also called *'interpreting'* God's voice).

3. How to gain a *deeper insight* and more *detail* about what God is showing us.

In general, I find that the interpreting part of the 'hearing from God' process is the bit that needs to be done with care and not be rushed.

TRYING TO
GET YOUR
ATTENTION

HEY THERE!

HOW GOD GETS OUR ATTENTION

"Moses saw that though the bush was on fire it did not burn up. So Moses thought, 'I will go over and see this strange sight– why the bush does not burn up.'"

Exodus 3:1-4

"Hey! I want to talk to you!" Have you ever seen a friend across the street or a room and wanted to get their attention? Depending on the circumstances, you might do different things to get them to look your way. You could call out their name, whistle at them or scrunch up a piece of paper and hurl it at them (hopefully your aim is decent).

There are many ways you can get someone's attention, aren't there? It's the same with God. As we walk with God we can expect Him to sometimes want to get our attention because of something He wants to talk to us about. How does He do this? Here are *some* (but not all) of the ways you can recognise that the Holy Spirit might be trying to get your attention.[1] Words seem to *leap* out or seem *highlighted* somehow (e.g. When you read the Bible).

1. Things feel like they've *slowed down* in a 'slow-motion-focus-on-this' type way.
2. It feels like someone has suddenly turned up, or even down, the *volume.*
3. Something happens and it feels like there's a *weightiness* to it.
4. Your heart or spirit burns within you (e.g. When Jesus appeared to the two disciples on the road to Emmaus and spoke to them they said, *"Were not our hearts burning within us while he talked with us on the road?"* Luke 24:32).

IDEA – DO

Live a life that makes it easy for God to get your attention.

1 Please note that I'm not describing something that literally happens, it's more that in your spirit you get a sense of these things taking place. The more we intentionally pay attention and listen to the Holy Spirit, the quicker we will be to sense when He's speaking to us in this manner.

AN INVITATION

WHEN GOD WANTS TO START A CONVERSATION

"And Moses said, 'Here I am.' "
Exodus 3:4

Often the things that get our attention are simply that; attention grabbers - such as the burning bush. The bush was not the message, it just got Moses' attention. The message followed as Moses made himself available. When God gets your attention, it's His way of saying, *"let's talk more".* It's a conversation starter.

Consider the humble egg. If I were to give you an intact but empty egg shell and a hardboiled egg and then asked you to tell me the difference between them, would you be able to? You probably would. One feels weightier and like it contains something, the other feels fragile and hollow. This is a bit like the difference between God's words and random or meaningless words.

What if I then asked you to tap the egg with a spoon. If you did this with the hollow egg, it wouldn't lead to anything. However if you did this with a hardboiled egg, you'd realise the shell was just the outer layer of what lies beneath. I call this the *'invitation revelation';* the attention-grabbing thing that God uses to tell you that He wants to start a conversation. Underneath that initial layer lies another layer to interact with. And as you continue to dig deeper, you discover the golden egg yolk - the core and heart of what God is communicating.

Let me use another analogy. If you've ever been to an art gallery you'll probably have noticed that many of the exhibits have beautiful, ornate frames. However, as elaborate as some of them can be, it's really not about the picture frame, is it? The frame is there to bring your focus and attention to what's central to the frame, the valuable masterpiece the artist has created.

When you feel that the Holy Spirit is getting your attention somehow, remember that the 'frame' or 'egg shell' is not the heart of the message (although it could be part of it). We need to tap, crack, peel and reveal to get the full message. And we do this by having a conversation with God, asking Him to give us understanding about what He's showing us.

IDEA – REFLECT

When God gets your attention, it's because He wants a conversation.

ASK
SEEK
KNOCK

CONVERSATION

GOD WANTS A DIALOGUE NOT A MONOLOGUE

"Ask and it will be given to you; seek and you will find; knock and the door will be opened to you."
Matthew 7:7

We are God's children, not His robots. God wants to have a conversation with you, not to download information to you like a computer programmer.

In Genesis 18:16-33 we see what a conversation with God looks like. God is angry with the people of Sodom because their *"sin is so grievous"* and so wants to wipe it out. But Abraham, God's friend, pleads on behalf of the righteous people. He asks whether God would spare the city for the sake of fifty righteous people. This is how God responds:

"The Lord said, 'If I find fifty righteous people in the city of Sodom, I will spare the whole place for their sake.'

Then Abraham spoke up again: 'Now that I have been so bold as to speak to the Lord, though I am nothing but dust and ashes, what if the number of the righteous is five less than fifty? Will you destroy the whole city for lack of five people?'

'If I find forty-five there,' he said, 'I will not destroy it.' "

The conversation progresses in a similar manner as Abraham pleads with God from forty, to thirty, to twenty, to ten righteous people.

Conversation is a vital part of healthy communication and relationship. When we want to know things or don't understand something, we can *ask questions* as part of that conversation. *Specific* questions help get specific answers. They help us get to the heart of what God is saying.

Ask what God is saying and He'll show you; *seek* His perspective and He'll give you understanding; *knock*, and the door to insight is opened.

IDEA – READ

Exodus 33:11

"The Lord would speak to Moses face to face, as one speaks to a friend."

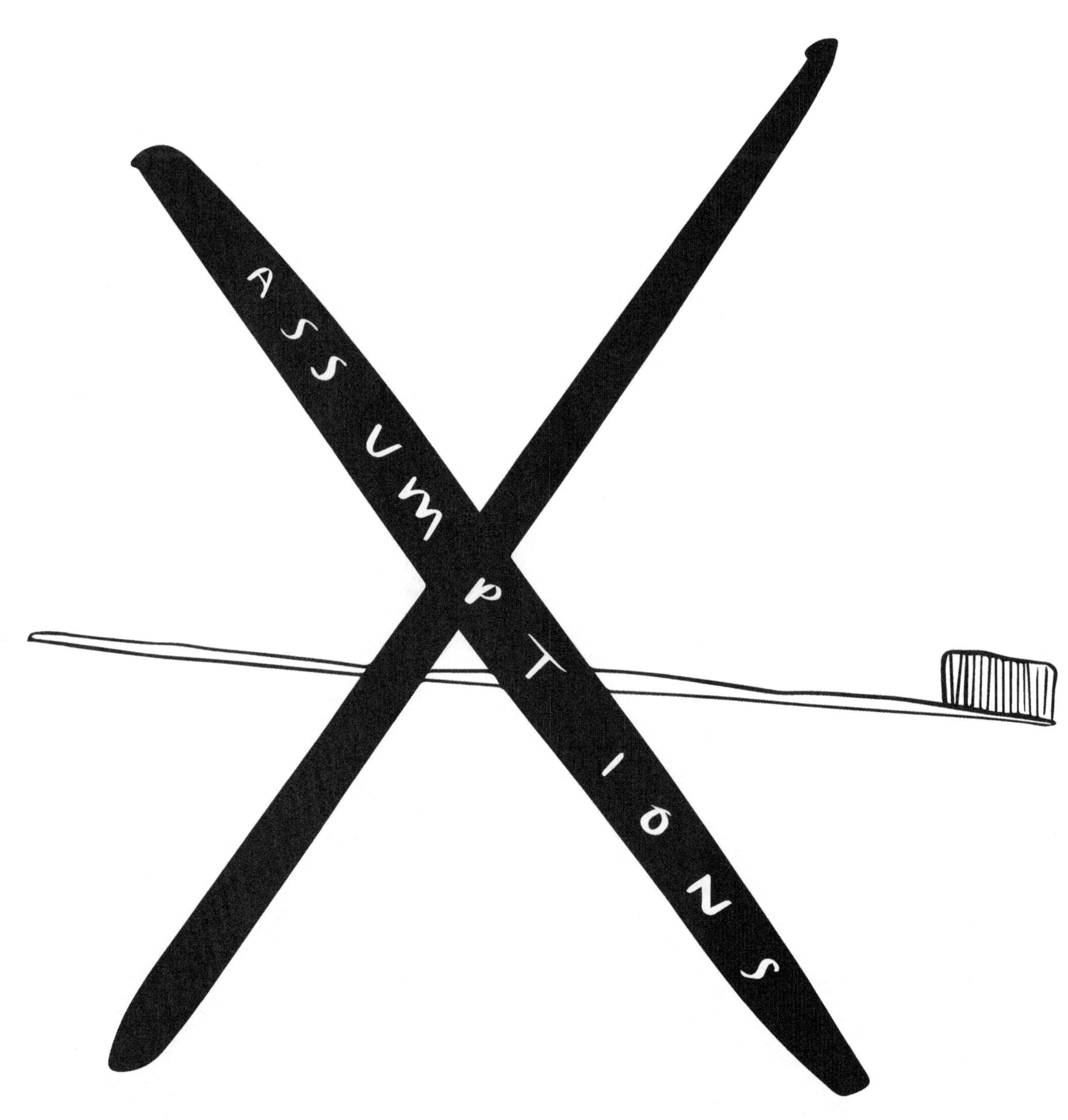
ASSUMPTIONS

UNDERSTANDING

WE NEED TO INTERPRET WHAT GOD IS SAYING

"Do not be wise in your own eyes"
Proverbs 3:7

In our house we have a 'toilet toothbrush'. An old toothbrush that's really handy for cleaning all the nooks and crannies in your bathroom that can gather grime, slime and mould.

A few years ago we had a wonderful, servant-hearted guest stay with us. She always does anything she can to help - if she sees a need, she'll meet it. On this occasion, she'd been helping me put the boys to bed and so updated me on their progress.

"They've just had a bath, they're in their pyjamas and they've had their teeth done."

I was delighted – we were well ahead of the bedtime schedule! But suddenly something dawned on me. The boys' toothbrushes were recharging in our bedroom.

Yes, you've guessed it. It turns out my boys had just had their teeth brushed by the bleach-soaked, mildew-eliminating, scum-destroying, bacteria-infested toothbrush.[1] The point of my story is this; to our guest a white toothbrush represented a tool for brushing teeth, but to me that same toothbrush represented quite a different thing. Although her intentions were exceptional, it would have been better if she'd *asked* me which toothbrush to use.

It's easy to make assumptions and jump to conclusions, assuming that our viewpoint is the correct one. Just as you'd seek to clarify and double-check with a friend, it's always a good idea to go back to God and ask whether we've interpreted and understood what He's saying correctly.

IDEA – REFLECT

The more you know someone, the less likely you are to misinterpret them – you know their heart as well as their head.

1 I admit the fact this happened was probably my fault. It wasn't wise to have stored it in the bathroom in the first place!

METAPHORICAL?

LITERAL OR METAPHORICAL?

SOMETIMES GOD SPEAKS IN SYMBOLIC WAYS

"His disciples asked him what this parable meant."
Luke 8:9

My youngest son, Rafe, is currently going through a phase where it's very important to him that you mean exactly what you say. If you say you'll be with him *"in a minute"*, he'll set a timer on his watch for 60 seconds and will expect you to be there when the timer goes off. He takes everything you say very literally.

But often what we say is descriptive, not literal.

Jesus spoke to people a lot through parables. Part of the process of understanding what God is saying is to work out whether what He's sharing with you is literal or metaphorical.

Imagine a lion popped into your head. What does it mean? My first place to go to would be the Bible. God is described as the Lion of Judah.[1] Is that what God wants to talk about? But who else is described like a lion in the Bible? The devil. *"Your enemy prowls around you like a roaring lion"*.[2] That's a very different meaning. Or maybe God wants to talk about something you associate a lion with - courage? Safaris? The England national football team? Or maybe it's about a memory you have.[3]

IDEA - THINK

Has God ever spoken to you in a symbolic or parabolic way?

1 Have a look in Revelation 5:5

2 See 1 Peter 5:8

3 Here's another example: supposing a pair of welly boots came into my mind. I have two pairs of wellies - a bright pink pair and a khaki green pair. The pink ones are waterproof, but the green pair leak and give me soggy socks. It would therefore be worth me asking God questions in order to understand what He was trying to say. *"Which pair is relevant, the waterproof pair or the leaking pair? Is the colour important and symbolic? Or are you wanting to say something about the brand name of the wellies, 'Hunter'?"*

A DISCO BALL

SOMETIMES THERE ARE LAYERS TO WHAT GOD IS SAYING

A disco ball is made up of hundreds of small mirrors, all angled slightly differently, reflecting light to several separate points. God's perspective is multi-faceted. Part of the purpose of asking questions is to see all the many layers and angles that might be hidden in a single thought, word or image. If we don't ask questions and for God's perspective, we could miss something He wants to show us.[1]

For example, one of these layers could be through *word association.*[2] I remember once an image of a sea bed covered in sand dollars[3] came into my head when praying for someone. As I asked God about it I felt the focus wasn't about the image, it was a play on words; sand *dollar.* God wanted to talk about money! I felt God wanted to reassure this person that they mustn't worry about their financial struggles, He would look after them.

Another time I'd been praying for someone and felt God was speaking through the image of a Lotus Seven sports car. The interesting thing was that just as I thought I'd shared everything, the word "anagram" came into my mind. This had never happened before. I wondered whether God was saying the word "Lotus Seven" was also an anagram. I discovered the words "Vessel Unto" can be made from Lotus Seven and that there's a Bible passage that contains the phrase.[4] I then felt God continue to share some things for this person through that passage.[5]

IDEA – REFLECT

In order to understand God's voice we need to learn to ask the right questions and seek out all the angles.

1 Don't get me wrong, there aren't always many layers. Sometimes God has one simple, straightforward message to share.

2 God did this with Jeremiah (Jeremiah 1:11)

3 A sand dollar is a type of sea urchin, I used to swim for them when I lived near warm sea!

4 2 Timothy 2:20-21 (KJV)

5 To you, deciphering anagrams may sound like hard work and effort. But remember God speaks to us individually. God knows that I love having fun in this kind of way and so He was speaking to me in a way that He knew that I'd enjoy!

ANNA'S
HUMMINGBIRD

GOD WINKS

LITTLE CONFIRMATIONS

"Along unfamiliar paths I will guide them"
Isaiah 42:16

Discerning God's voice from the other chatter in our head can require perseverance. At times you might need encouragement. Sometimes if I feel like I could do with some reassurance, I ask God for a little 'wink' or 'thumbs up' from Him to show me that I'm on the right track.

In the Bible, animals and their associated characteristics are often used symbolically.[1] I once did an exercise where we were invited to ask God which animal we had similarities with. When I did this, a hummingbird came into my mind. I didn't know much about them so I began to research them. As I did, I felt God highlight certain relevant things (some specific to me, some general for all). For example, hummingbirds have extremely fast metabolisms. They therefore need to feed constantly and rest frequently. I felt God was saying that I too needed to be filled afresh every day with His Spirit. Spending time at rest with Him was also really important.

There were more specific things I felt like God was saying to me personally, but in the end I really wanted a bit of reassurance that I wasn't making it all up. So I asked for a 'wink'. Nothing entered my mind immediately but at the end of my reading, I noticed a list of all the different kinds of hummingbird species. And there it was, a species called, *"Calypte anna"* or *"Anna's Hummingbird"*. To me this was a little wink that I was hearing correctly.[2]

IDEA – REFLECT

Have you ever experienced a God wink?

1 For example, God is compared to an eagle (Exodus 19:4), a lamb (Isaiah 53:7) and a lion (Revelation 5:5).

2 WARNING! Beware of 'blinks'! Sometimes we might think certain things are from God because we *want* them to mean something even though they actually *don't*. ie. We see what we want to see and read too much into things. The way we learn the difference between God winks and blinks is by asking God for discernment and wisdom (and by asking trustworthy people).

UNFORCED

THERE'S AN EASE & FLOW TO GOD'S VOICE

"Whoever believes in me, as Scripture has said, rivers of living water will flow from within them."
John 7:38

When I start to ask God questions I often find that (if it is indeed God's voice) there's an ease and *flow-like momentum* to the conversation (ie. questions and answers) or flow of thought that doesn't feel forced or fabricated. The questions and answers seem to flow like waves or 'bubble up' like spring water, carrying with them a discernible 'freshness'. This is one of the ways I recognise that something is from God.

Let me describe this another way. I love jigsaw puzzles.[1] As you'll probably know, sometimes there can be many similar shaped or coloured pieces in a puzzle which can make it hard to work out which one is right. However when you find it, the real piece just slots into place with little or no effort needed; any other piece requires a certain amount of force. This is another way of describing the flow that I mentioned before.

When I'm trying to work out which one of the many different voices, thoughts and pictures that come into my head are actually from God, it's a bit like taking hold of different puzzle pieces and trying them out. God's voice seems to *'connect'* or *'click'* into place with my spirit with a *'rightness'* that doesn't happen with the other thoughts and pictures I have.

IDEA – REMEMBER

Hearing God's voice is a journey of growth and we will learn through trial and error!

1 They're one of the only things that help me completely switch off and relax.

A JOURNEY

GROWING THROUGH PERSONAL EXPERIENCE

Recognising God's voice for yourself will involve a *personal process.*

It's a *relational* journey that will take place over time and will involve:

1. Lots of experience
2. Making mistakes

Your journey will look different to others, but it needs to be yours.

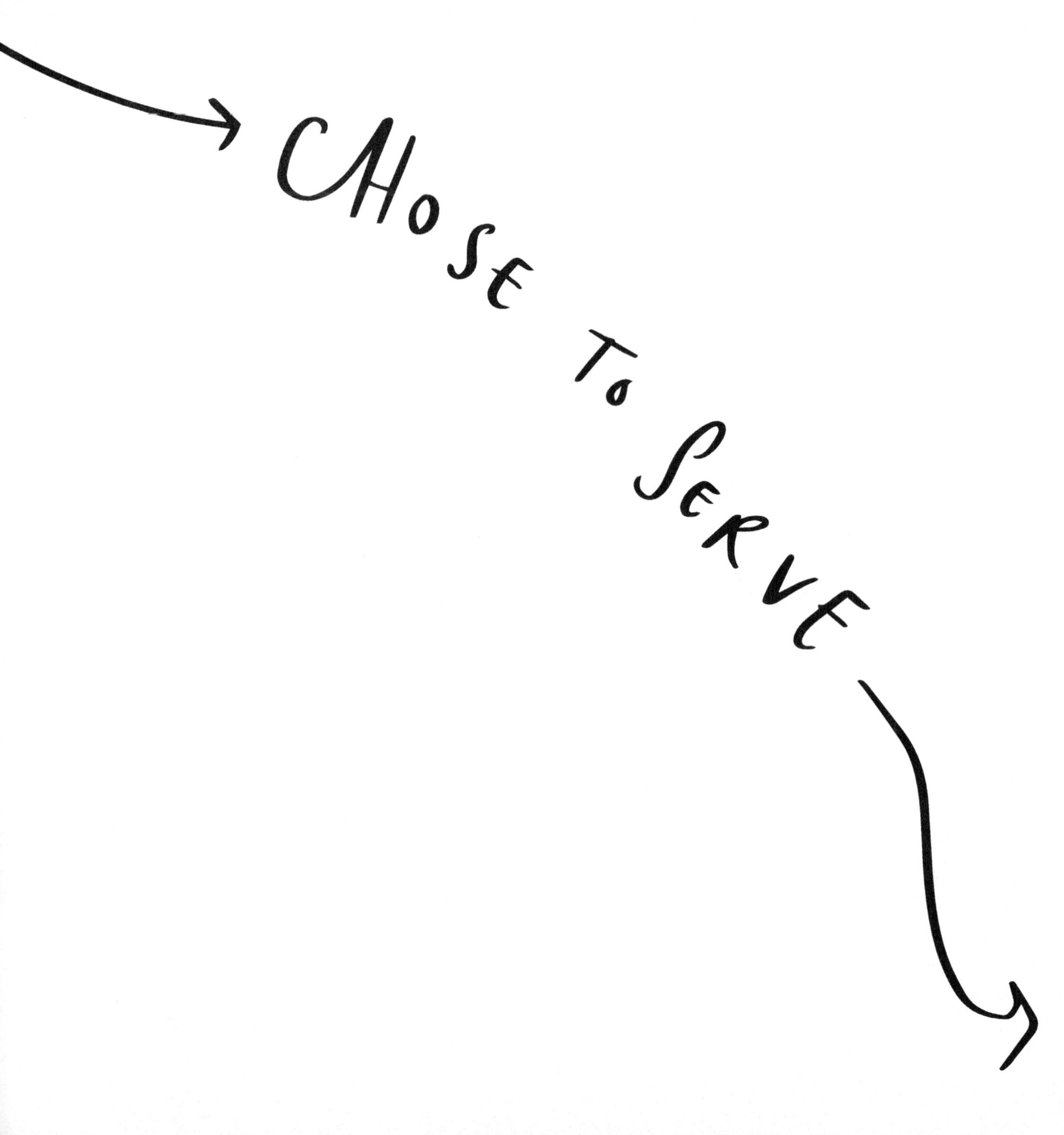
CHOSE TO SERVE

HIDDEN SERVICE

GOD TRAINS US IN UNSEEN PLACES

"For even the Son of Man did not come to be served, but to serve."
Mark 10:45

Jesus calls us to be ambassadors to the world around us as we walk with ongoing connection to Him. What does this journey and lifestyle look like? Where do we begin?

Jesus began His ministry when he was about thirty years old.[1] Besides the account of Jesus' birth and infancy, there is only one account in the Bible about his childhood. That's when He was in the temple courts of Jerusalem when he was 12 years old, amazing his teachers with his knowledge of the Scriptures.[2] At the end of the account we're then told that Jesus went back with His parents to Nazareth *"and was obedient to them".* There in Nazareth, from age 12 to 30, *"Jesus grew in wisdom and stature, and in favour with God and men".*

That's it.

That's all the detail we get from the Bible about what Jesus did for all those early years. We do, however, know that He was a carpenter's son, so he was most likely serving His earthy father in the area of carpentry. This was obviously not His main purpose of coming to the earth. But I believe that as Jesus chose to serve in this way, His Heavenly Father was training Him how to live everyday life responding to His voice.

It's often in the unseen place of hidden service that God shapes us and trains us, through relationship, to recognise His heart and voice.

IDEA – REFLECT

Serving others is a great way to hear from God.

Where are you serving?

1 See Luke 3:23

2 Also look at Luke 2:41-52

MANY WON'T
KNOW YOUR NAME
BUT I WILL
AND THAT'S WHAT
MATTERS

TRUE IDENTITY

IT'S IMPORTANT WE KNOW WHO WE ARE

"Whatever you do, work at it with all your heart, as working for the Lord, not for human masters"
Colossians 3:23

As a child, I always knew I wanted to discover stuff. In the end, I decided to study neuroscience.[1] I thought the brain was the greatest area of unknown! So I spent four years doing an undergraduate degree, a year of work experience, three years doing a PhD and finally five years of research.

At this point everything changed.

My husband was asked to lead our church and we had our first child. After much discussion and prayer, we decided I should take a break from academia to focus on family. In my mind, this was a temporary break, however each time I thought about going back to work, I felt God say, "no". I was confused by this. I'd invested so much in my career, now I was committing 'career suicide'.

But God knew what He was doing. One of the things He showed me was that He needed to take away everything that had become too much a part of my identity, that shouldn't have been.

"Once you were known as Dr. Goodman, but now you'll be "Fin's mum". Many won't know your name, but I will and that's what matters. Most people won't know you have a degree or PhD. But that doesn't matter - I qualify you, not your qualifications. You'll carry out the lowest paid jobs, but won't get paid. How much you earn does not dictate your worth, I do. No-one may notice what you do, but I will. Do it for me, an audience of one."

That experience changed me. It was during this time - when I was walking in the repetitive, everyday, hidden tasks of life - that God began teaching me what His voice sounds like and what it meant to live life as His child.

IDEA – REFLECT

Being bored is really great if it causes us to turn our listening attention towards God!

1 I wanted to be an archaeologist, a palaeontologist and a forensic scientist.

SMALL BEGINNINGS

GROWTH & MATURITY TAKES TIME

"The kingdom of heaven is like a mustard seed, which a man took and planted in his field. Though it is the smallest of all seeds, yet when it grows, it is the largest of garden plants and becomes a tree, so that the birds come and perch in its branches."
Matthew 13:31-32

The largest tree in the world is a giant sequoia. It's called General Sherman[1] and it's huge - about 52,500 cubic feet in volume.[2]

Sometimes when we look at a tree like that and marvel with great wonder, we forget that it's also 2,000 years old and at one point it was only a seed. A seed that became a seedling, which grew into a sapling and then slowly over time, much time, became a small tree, then a larger one.

But that took time.

Sometimes we may come across people who hear from God in ways that seem to be incredibly profound and clear. We look at them and think, *"If only I could hear God like that!"*

We assume they've always been able to hear like that and that it's come easily and naturally to them without any work or effort. But the truth is, it probably took a long time to get to that point.

But the good news is, you too can grow - if you're willing to intentionally invest in your walk and relationship with God, which is the soil that enables that growth.

IDEA – REFLECT

Learning to hear God's voice will take time.

Like growing a seed.

1 Also called the Sequoiadendron giganteum. You can find it in California's Sequoia National Park.

2 That's the equivalent of more than half the volume of an Olympic-size swimming pool.

FIXED

GROWTH

GROWTH MINDSET

MATURITY REQUIRES INVESTMENT

"He who began a good work in you will carry it on to completion until the day of Christ Jesus."
Philippians 1:6

If I always copied someone else's work and never did my own homework, I'd never really learn or reach my own personal potential.

True growth and maturity cannot be copied or borrowed.

At my son's school they talk about the different learning mindsets; a *fixed* or a *growth mindset.*[1]

In a fixed mindset, people believe their qualities are fixed and cannot change. They believe talent alone leads to success and effort is not required.

Alternatively, in a growth mindset, people believe that their learning and intelligence can grow with time and experience. When people believe this, they realise that their effort has an effect on their success, so they put in extra time, leading to higher performance.

I think that the concept of growth mindset is relevant to us in our walk with God. As His children we are created to (or have the 'spiritual DNA' for) hearing God's voice. However, that doesn't mean we don't need to put some effort in. We do. It's called *investment.* It's called *relationship.*

The more time you spend with God, the better you'll be at working out when He's speaking and what He's saying.

IDEA – REFLECT

How much time do you spend intentionally investing in your relationship with God?

1 Dweck, C. S. (2006). Mindset: The new psychology of success. New York: Random House.

WHEN NOT IF

PRACTICE

THE IMPORTANCE OF TRIAL & ERROR

"Although a righteous person may fall seven times, he gets up again"
Proverbs 24:16

In order for an athlete to become an Olympian, that person needs to practice. A lot. In order to be good at anything, you need to practice, a lot.[1]

Hearing God's voice is no exception.

In order to hear the Father's voice more clearly we need to be *intentional*. It's not that we need to strive to hear God's voice, but we do need to regularly *listen* and *test* out what we're hearing so we can discern His voice.

When you are learning something you often go through a period of *trial and error.* You make a bunch of mistakes and only then do you excel *after* you've made mistakes.

When my son got his first bicycle, we first put stabilisers on it until we thought he was ready, then we took them off and took him to ride on the grass by the play park so that when, not if, he fell, he wouldn't get hurt.

We need to *expect* to get it wrong sometimes but don't give up! Remain teachable. Mistakes are an important part of any growth process. If you *learn* from your mistakes, you will grow and get better!

Keep humbly stepping out, even if your steps are only small. Recognising God's voice will get easier with time and experience.

IDEA – REFLECT

What mistakes have you learnt from recently in your walk with God?

1 The other thing Olympic athletes do as part of their training is to practice with a lot of noise around them. This is so they can learn to focus and not be distracted by anything on the big day. Trying to intentionally hear God's voice in different environments e.g. whilst out shopping, in a restaurant, whilst at the dentist, is a great form of discipline and will help us grow.

	KNOWLEDGE	SKILL
1	? ? ? ? UNAWARE	? ? ? ?
2	AWARE	! ? ! ? ! ?
3		PRACTICE
4		EASY!

PERSEVERE

GROWING IN COMPETENCE

"Let us run with perseverance the race marked out for us"
Hebrews 12:1

Being certain of God's voice becomes easier with practice. The more you spend time with Him and in Scripture, the clearer His voice will become. The more you listen, the more you'll learn and grow. Use any sense of discouragement to push through and keep going. Persevere!

I've found *"The four levels of teaching"* model helpful in understanding the stages of learning. This looks like the following:[1]

1. *Unconscious Incompetence* – When you aren't aware that a skill or knowledge gap exists.
2. *Conscious Incompetence* – You're aware of a skill or knowledge gap and understand the importance of acquiring the new skill. Learning can now begin.
3. *Conscious Competence* – When you know how to use the skill or perform the task, but doing so requires practice, conscious thought and hard work.
4. *Unconscious Competence* – When you have enough experience that you can perform the skill unconsciously.

When it comes to hearing God's voice, it looks like this:

1. When we aren't aware that we need to learn how to grow in recognising God's voice.
2. When you realise you need to learn how to recognise how God is speaking to you.
3. Intentionally practising hearing from God.
4. You're so used to talking and listening to God that you're not always aware that you're having a conversation with Him, it's just an ongoing exchange of minds and hearts[2].

When you practice a lot, the intentional becomes natural.

IDEA – THINK

Where do you think you are on the competency scale?

1 Broadwell, Martin M. (20 February 1969). "Teaching for learning (XVI)"

2 Perhaps this is something we'll never truly achieve until we're with Him in eternity, but we can still aim for it!

WHAT

KITCHEN UTENSIL

(INSERT RANDOM RIDICULOUS OBJECT!)

AM I LIKE?

LOW-COST EXPERIENCE

BEHIND CLOSED DOORS, LOW-RISK PRACTISING

Part of my personal journey in recognising God's voice involved a time of asking God lots of child-like, low-cost, low-risk questions. I'm rather embarrassed sharing them with you now, because they will seem ridiculous. However, my motivation was simply to learn, discern and grow. God is kind and knows our heart. I don't think He minds being asked silly questions if our intentions are pure.[1] God meets us where we're at and then encourages us to take the next step forward.

I'd ask my questions and wait for the response so that I could work out what it sounded like when God's thoughts came into my head, compared to when it was just my own. For example:[2]

1. *"What kitchen utensil am I like?"* [An image of a tin opener enters my mind.]
   "Why?" [A thought pops into my mind: *"Sometimes I'll use you to unlock and reveal things I've placed in people."*]

2. *"What vehicle am I like?"* [Image of a bulldozer comes into my head]
   "Why?" [I immediately remember that it helps clear away rubble so new structures can be built.]

3. *"What semi-precious stone am I like?"* [The word *"Agate"* comes into my head.]
   "Why?" [I felt that the focus was on the word. *"It's a play on words: 'A Gate.' You are like a gate between heaven and earth because my Spirit is in you."*]

What I learnt was that, for me, a sense of understanding entered my thoughts that I somehow knew hadn't come from within me. I could just tell the thought was different than my own. It was subtle, but as I practised, it got easier to tell the difference.

IDEA – DO

What low-risk step can you take today?

1 Don't wait until you're in emergency, high-risk or very public situations before you start the journey of listening for God's voice. Gain experience listening during your own private time when the cost is low and the stakes aren't high!

2 God can speak through anything. In the Bible He literally spoke through a donkey (Read Numbers 22 - it's a great story.)

"WHEN I LOOK AT YOU, I SEE JESUS"

HIDDEN WITH CHRIST

GOD'S TRUTH SPOKEN THROUGH NATURE

"I have been crucified with Christ and I no longer live, but Christ lives in me."
Galatians 2:20

I was in the garden one hot summer's afternoon and being inspired by all the nature around me I asked, *"When you look at me, what do you see? What flower am I like?"* Again, writing it down now is embarrassing, but once again God patiently humoured my heart to learn.

The image of a passion fruit flower entered my mind. I was delighted, assuming this was because I was somehow 'exotic and unique' in the way that He designed me! But as that thought, my thought, danced through my mind, I got the impression that I was wrong about my egotistical interpretation. Knowing nothing further about the flower and not feeling that God was giving me any more details about it, I went off to research it.What I found was very humbling.

The 'passion' in 'passion flower' refers to the passion of Jesus in Christian theology. Its history comes from Spanish Christian missionaries who adopted the unique physical structures of this plant as symbols of the suffering and sacrifice experienced by Jesus before His crucifixion. In Spain, it's known as *"Christ's thorn"* and other names given throughout Europe all reference Jesus.

So what I felt like God the Father was showing me was this: *"When I look at you, I see Jesus."*

It was simple, beautiful and profound.

IDEA - READ

Colossians 3:3

"For you died, and your life is now hidden with Christ in God"

BRICK

GREEN

CHILD-LIKE TRUST

DON'T OVERCOMPLICATE THINGS

"Trust in the Lord with all your heart and lean not on your own understanding"

Proverbs 3:5

I've admitted to you that my questions were child-like and possibly naive. Children have a wonderful, trusting way of taking things at face value. Sometimes adults can complicate things unnecessarily. When I've taught children on this subject, they seem to effortlessly be able to hear from God.

I was sharing my question asking process with my son and suggested that he might like to do something similar. He wondered about asking God to speak to him through colour and so we went with that. After a few seconds of waiting he replied with the following:

"I have it! I got the colour 'brick green.'" I was puzzled. I'd never heard of 'brick green'.

"Don't you mean, 'brick red'?" I asked. *"No,"* he replied. *"It's brick green."*

"Well, what does that mean?" I wondered out loud, still not knowing what to make of it.

"God says He's going to use me to build life - the brick bit is about building, the green bit represents life."

How wonderful. A new colour that made no sense to me, was given to my son to communicate how God was going to use him to bring life wherever he went. And this is, of course, what all Christians are called to do.

I pondered about this afterwards and realised if God had put that colour in my head, I would have probably dismissed it as nonsensical - 'there's no such thing!' - but my son just accepted and received it.

IDEA – REFLECT

Having a child-like attitude of trust opens the door to God speaking to us without our imposed limits.

RECORD YOUR JOURNEY

KEEP TRACK OF YOUR ADVENTURE

"Write in a book all the words I have spoken to you."
Jeremiah 30:2

I think it's a great idea to record your journey so you can go back and reflect on how things have changed and what you've learnt.[1] You can write a journal, keep notes on your phone, draw pictures – whatever works best for you, just somehow keep track so you can celebrate your progress. Over the months and years we can quickly forget how far we've come and it's good to keep encouraging yourself, especially when you feel like you haven't gone anywhere.

Having a record of what you have said will also help you grow faster. You'll be able to work out where you've been getting things right and where you've got things wrong.

I try to keep a record using who, what, how, when and where questions. For example: *How do I feel God communicated with me? How confident do I feel that it was God? How long did I spend talking to God about this? Do I need to ask any more questions? Did the conversation flow or did it feel forced? Do I need to do anything about what I feel God is saying? Could I have got the interpretation wrong? How did I feel when God was speaking? Can I get feedback somehow?*

Be kind and be patient with yourself and remember this is a process. God not only wants to teach you how to recognise His voice, but He also wants to teach you about His nature.[2]

Every small step in the right direction counts, keep walking!

IDEA – DO

Start a record of your journey today.

1 I wouldn't have been able to write this book if I hadn't done that. So many things I thought I'd never forget, I had!

2 One of the things I've discovered about God's nature is that He has a sense of humour. Once when praying for a group of people, I felt God speak through the image of a banana. Bananas contain a hormone that causes its own ripening and the ripening of the fruit around it. God often works through His people to bring about a maturing and ripening in others – I felt God say, *"You're a bunch of bananas!"* It made me laugh.

WHAT DO YOU THINK GOD IS SAYING?

IN ONE WORD?

IN ONE SENTENCE?

HOW DID THIS INFORMATION COME TO YOU?

A PICTURE? A THOUGHT? A BIBLE VERSE?

COULD THERE BE ANOTHER WAY OF INTERPRETING WHAT YOU FEEL GOD SAYING?

WAS THERE A **FLOW** WITH HOW IT CAME TO YOU?

HOW DO YOU **FEEL?**

PEACEFUL? UNEASY? HOPEFUL? ENCOURAGED? WAS THERE A BOUNCE IN YOUR SPIRIT?

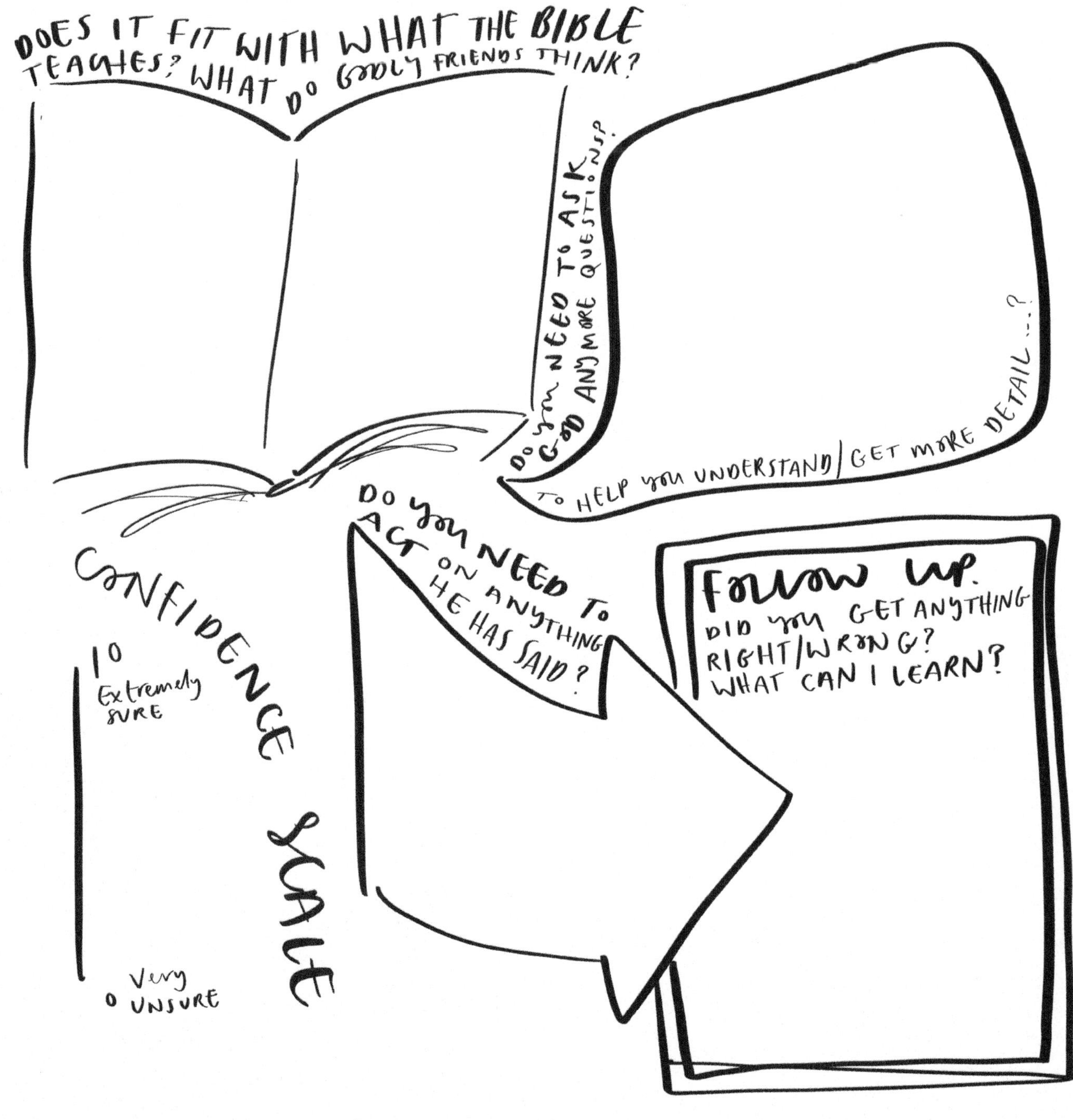
DOES IT FIT WITH WHAT THE BIBLE TEACHES? WHAT DO GODLY FRIENDS THINK?
DO YOU NEED TO ASK GOD ANYMORE QUESTIONS?
TO HELP YOU UNDERSTAND/GET MORE DETAIL...?
DO YOU NEED TO ACT ON ANYTHING HE HAS SAID?
FOLLOW UP.
DID YOU GET ANYTHING RIGHT/WRONG?
WHAT CAN I LEARN?
CONFIDENCE SCALE
10 Extremely SURE
0 Very UNSURE

- PART 2 -

GOD CAN SPEAK THROUGH YOU

TO CONNECT WITH OTHERS

WHY DOES HE USE US?

WHEN GOD WANTS TO USE YOU TO CONNECT WITH OTHERS

Why would God want to use us to connect to others and why should we want to be used by God in this way?

I'd like to suggest two main reasons:

1. To encourage and build up the Church, God's family.

2. To reach out to God's lost children.

The motivation behind both of these reasons is the same – love. God wants to express His love through you.

KALEIDOSCOPE CHURCH

THE GLORIOUSLY VARIED BODY OF CHRIST

"So in Christ we, though many, form one body, and each member belongs to all the others. We have different gifts, according to the grace given to each of us."

Romans 12:4–6

I watched the very first brick being laid on our housing development. One of the things that struck me as I watched the houses being built was just how many people were involved. Surveyors, engineers, architects, bricklayers, electricians, plumbers, plasterers, and decorators. Each person was vital and each job relied on the support and work of another.

This is a bit like the Body of Christ. The Holy Spirit gives us each different gifts in order to build up the church. Every person is needed - no single person can do it all by themselves. And that's how Jesus intended it to be.

Growing up abroad meant we didn't really have access to chocolate and the chocolate we did have tasted odd. One of my favourite memories was coming back to the UK and opening a whole tin of Quality Street chocolates. As a little girl, it looked like a treasure chest full of multi-coloured jewels, all shining brightly in their different shapes and sizes. I'd plunge my face into the centre of the tin and inhale deeply, filling my nostrils with all the aromas, from coconut to caramel.

For me, those Quality Streets are a bit like the gifts of the Spirit. Each gift offers up a different flavour; a different colour that makes the church so varied and beautiful when shining on display together.[1]

IDEA – READ

1 Corinthians 12.

What gifts of the Spirit do you think you've been given?

1 I shared this analogy at Sunday school during one session and handed around a full tin and each child got to pick their own chocolate. Much to their dismay (especially given how much time they'd spent making their choices), I then asked them to give their chocolate to the person next to them. The gifts of the Spirit are "for the common good"; they're meant to be shared!

ASK

GIFT of PROPHECY

THE CHURCH

THE CHURCH

THE CHURCH

THE CHURCH

ENCOURAGE

STRENGTH

COMFORT

POWERFUL PROPHECY

HEARING & SHARING GOD'S WORDS

"To each one the manifestation of the Spirit is given for the common good. To one there is given through the Spirit a message of wisdom... to another prophecy."
1 Corinthians 12: 7–10

Prophecy is one of the free gifts of the Spirit.[1] It means to be inspired by God to see and speak what He's seeing and speaking now. This could be about the past, present or future.

1 Corinthians 14:1 says, *"Follow the way of love and eagerly desire gifts of the Spirit, especially prophecy."* But why should we want to deeply desire to speak what God is speaking now? What is the primary purpose of prophecy?

Those are great questions. The answer lies here:

"The one who prophesies speaks to people for their strengthening, encouraging and comfort. Anyone who speaks in a tongue edifies themselves, but the one who prophesies edifies the church."[2]

Prophecy is a powerful gift.

One birthday, my son was desperate for a particular Thunderbirds rocket:

"Please can I have Thunderbird 3 for my birthday? It can fly and be a drill. It plays a countdown sequence when it takes off and smoke comes out! It's only £39.99 and you can get it from Amazon. All my friends will really enjoy playing with it!"

This is similar to what Paul is saying; *Eagerly* desire the gift of prophecy! It's a *free* gift from the Holy Spirit! It's such a *powerful* tool for building up the church. *Everyone* will benefit!

IDEA – REFLECT

God wants us to hear His words so that His church can grow healthy and strong.

1 It comes from a Greek word that means to speak forth by divine inspiration.

2 1 Corinthians 14: 3-4

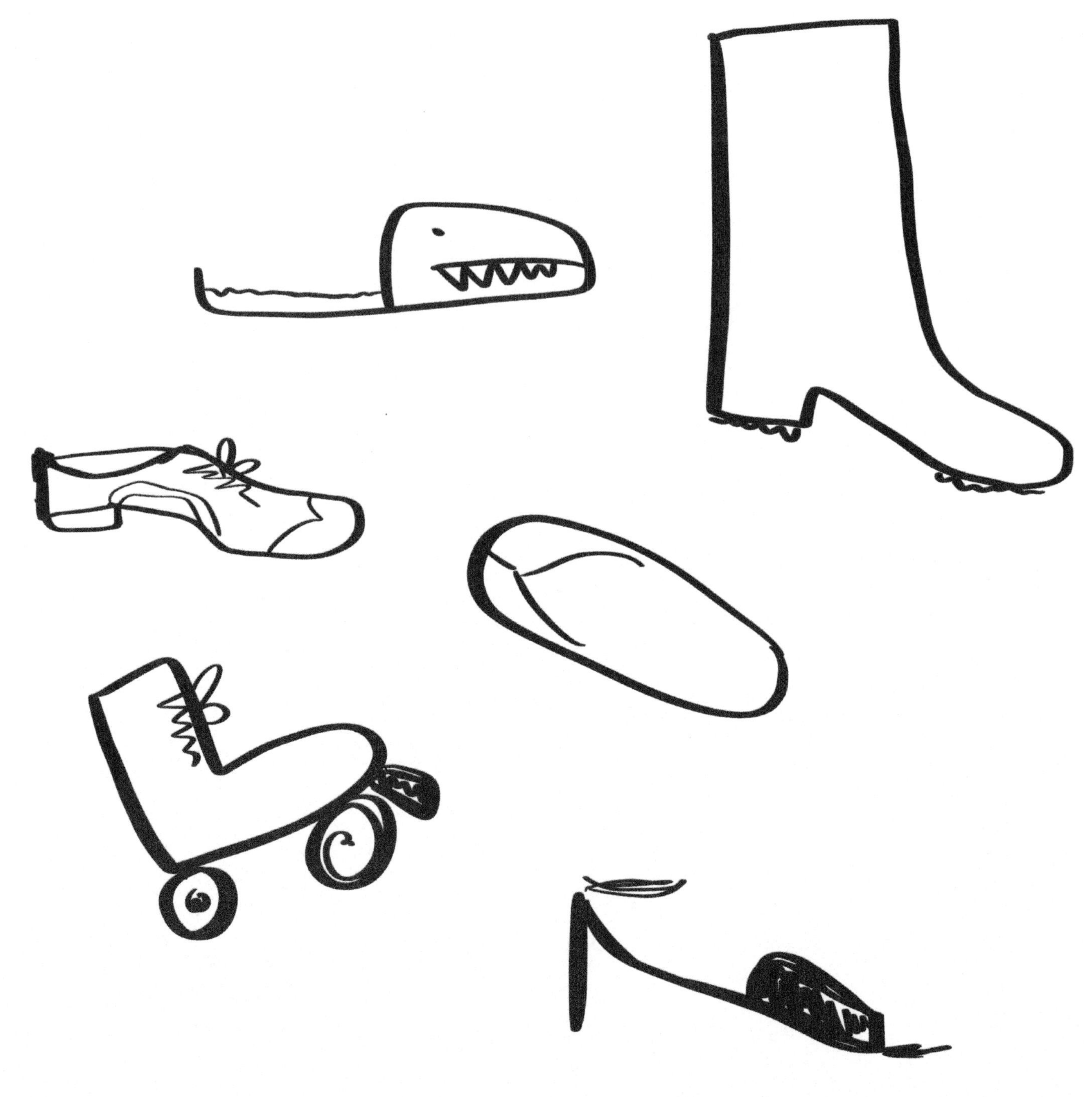

AN INVITATION

REPRESENTING JESUS TO OTHERS

"We are therefore Christ's ambassadors, as though God were making his appeal through us. We implore you on Christ's behalf: Be reconciled to God."
2 Corinthians 5:20

Sometimes God will want to speak through you in order to reach out to those who don't yet know Him. God's Words from God's heart are an invitation, they point people to Jesus, inviting them into a relationship with Him.

I once did a creative workshop that was aimed at helping you work out the 'sound' of God's voice. One of the activities involved asking God to put into your mind a pair of shoes. Once a pair entered your mind, you were then encouraged to ask God questions about what He wanted to say through them.

I thought this was a fun exercise and have actually asked God this question many times at different points in my life. Different shoes seem to come into my mind depending on what God seems to be focusing on.[1]

However, what recently came into my mind impacted me the most. As I prayed, I saw a pair of sandals. They were well-used, leather, men's sandals that were obviously far too big for me. I didn't immediately understand their relevance and so I asked Jesus what they meant. The reply I heard was soft, but firm.

"They're my sandals, Anna. I'm giving them to you. I want you to remember that everywhere you walk, I walk there with you. Represent me well."

IDEA – REFLECT

We represent Jesus well to others when we do the things He would do and say the things He would say.

1 For example, at one point some crocodile slippers entered my mind, along with the phrase: *"Keep things snappy!"* I felt God was encouraging me to be more focused and disciplined in what I shared with others because I was tending to waffle a bit!

GOD'S PERSPECTIVE

SEEING THROUGH GOD'S EYES

"The Lord does not look at the things people look at. People look at the outward appearance, but the Lord looks at the heart."
1 Samuel 16:7

The world saw David as a young shepherd boy, but God saw a King. We need God's perspective.

I once kept bumping into a particular person and felt God was encouraging me to get to know them. Over the weeks as we chatted, I discovered that she was part of a group, *The Scorpions.*[1] This concerned me because I knew some of the stuff the group got up to and that it was involved in some dark and sinister things.

One day she invited me to her house. At first I wondered whether this was a wise thing to do. However, my godly friends reminded me that I didn't need to be afraid because God's Spirit was in me and He was more powerful than any darkness in this world.[2]

The day I was due to go over to her house, I got in touch with my friends to ask them to pray for me because I was *"about to go over to The Scorpion's house".*

But as soon as I'd sent out that message, I felt a deep sadness in my heart that I knew was not my own. *"God, what's wrong?"* I asked. *"I feel like I've upset you somehow."* As soon as I'd said that, a reply seemed to bounce back in my heart.

"Can you please stop calling her a Scorpion? That's not her identity. That's not how I see her and who I created her to be."

We need God's perspective.

IDEA – READ

2 Corinthians 5:16

"From now on, therefore, we regard no one according to the flesh."

1 Not the real name.

2 1 John 4:4 is a great passage to remind yourself of if you ever get scared about the darkness in this world.

How Do I Share God's Heart?

Passing On a Message Well

So far we have discussed what prophecy is (seeing what God sees, saying what God says) and why we should do it (God encourages us to).

Now I want to help us think through the following question:

How can I most clearly, effectively and lovingly communicate what I feel like God is saying to others?

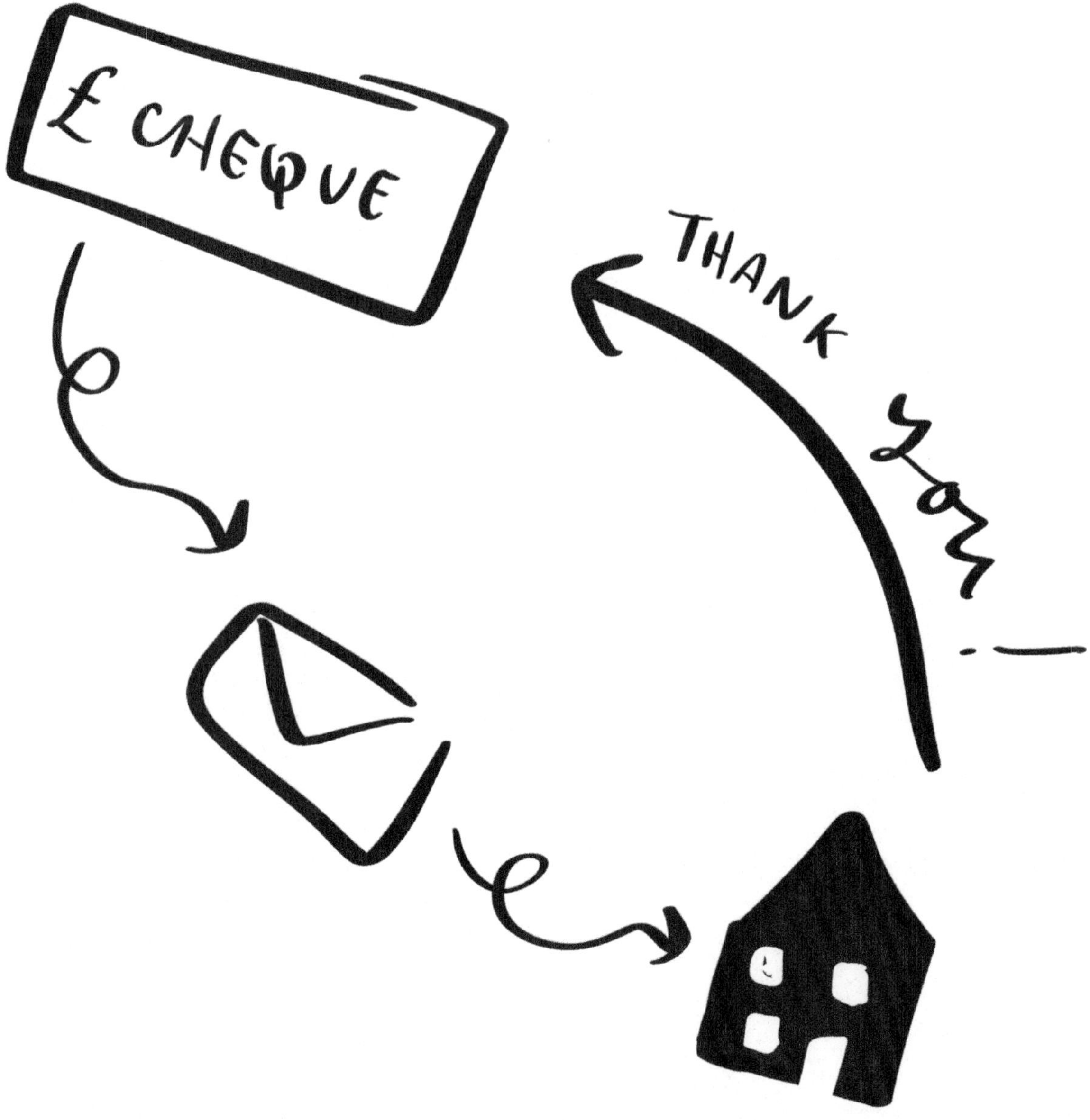

£ CHEQUE

THANK you

DELIVERY PEOPLE

WE ARE GOD'S MESSENGERS

"How beautiful are the feet of those who bring good news!"
Romans 10:15

We have the privilege of having access and being connected to the Father's heart and to the heart of men. When we are willing to love and serve them both, we are able to reach and grab what the Father wants to give them and deliver it into the hearts of the children.

I like the description of being like God's postal person. God gives you a 'message/letter/present' to give to the person He's addressed it to. You simply do your job and deliver it.

Sometimes prophecy is about delivering a 'gift' from God, but sometimes it's about showing you a gift He's *already* given someone and how to unwrap it.

Another analogy is being like a waiter or waitress. The chef[1] prepares the food, the waiter delivers it and the customer gets to enjoy the meal! God loves to feed us (and others) with His life-giving words.

"The Sovereign Lord has given me a well-instructed tongue, to know the word that sustains the weary. He wakens me morning by morning, wakens my ear to listen like one being instructed."[2]

IDEA – DO

Ask God for something to share with someone who feels weary and needs encouragement.

---

1 My brother is head chef at a hotel in Gothenburg, Sweden. Just like God, he takes great care in what he creates. It is beautiful.

2 Isaiah 50:4

LOVE

DELIVERY PACKAGE

HOW TO SHARE GOD'S WORDS

Tiny tweets, Instagram images, memorable memes, punchy podcasts, interesting infographics, provocative posts, sobering status updates, song samples. The variety is great and information can be communicated in a multitude of different shapes and sizes.

When we feel like God wants us to share something, one of the questions we need to ask Him is, *"How?"*

Should it be shared *publicly* or *privately?* In *written form* or *verbally?* Is a specific *Bible reference* all that's needed? Will a *drawing* most clearly convey what God is saying? Should I sing it,[1] say it, or strategically *pray it?* I'm afraid I can't give you the answer to this, but God can![2]

The main thing to keep in mind is that whatever we do, whatever we say, however we say it, the delivery package should always be *honouring, respectful* and above all, *loving.*

A few years ago I went to a conference where the guest speaker was sharing very specific words from God with people. A friend of mine was there and one of the 'words from God' that were given exactly described her with extraordinary detail. I was amazed. But I was also saddened. Although what he shared was very impressive, the Father heart of God didn't seem to come through. After the meeting, I went over to my friend and shared with the excitement. Interestingly, however, without me mentioning anything, she went on to say that although she admitted that everything he said was incredibly detailed, she felt like he had just *talked at her.* She was given a delivery, but that package didn't contain love.

IDEA – REFLECT

Love is always the key 'take-home' message to deliver.

1 I once felt God wanted me to sing what He was saying over the church. I was the most *terrifying* thing I've ever done.

2 I'd like to emphasise again at this point that whatever we do and say must be rooted and grounded in Scripture. As much as possible, ask the Holy Spirit to help provide you with Bible references to strengthen and back up what you're saying.

YOU
ARE
THE
MESSAGE

YOU ARE THE MESSAGE

EVERY PART OF YOU IS COMMUNICATING SOMETHING

"My command is this: Love each other as I have loved you."
John 15:12

To communicate God's heart effectively, our whole body, not just our words, should reflect the Father. This includes our tone of voice and body language. The message isn't simply your words - *you* are the message.[1]

Part of my research for writing this book involved reading a book called, *"How to get your point across in 30 seconds - or less"* by Milo Frank. He points out that how you say something is often more important than what you say and that you're communicating a message as soon as a person sees you whether you utter a word or not. Your body talks when your mouth doesn't, so make sure it's saying the right things.[2]

I watched a TEDx talk on public speaking and communication recently.[3] In it the presenter did a clever demonstration. He spoke for a solid minute, but everything he said he contradicted with his body language. At the end of the talk you realised that you'd only listened to his body language, which said exactly the opposite of his verbal message.

Our words and body language therefore need to be consistent in communicating the same message - love.

IDEA - REFLECT

How aware are you of your non-verbal communication?

Try to become more aware of your body language.

---

1 When my son was learning to walk, I'd hold him up but he actually took the steps. Active participation from us both was necessary. Similarly, when God uses you, *both* you and God will come through in the message.

2 1 Corinthians 14:23 says, *"The spirits of prophets are subject to the control of prophets".* You're always in control of what you say and how you say it. Jesus was always His natural self when He ministered. Don't be weird. Just be normal when you speak.

3 *"The 110 techniques of communication and public speaking"* by David JP Phillips (it's on YouTube and it's 16:51 mins long.)

JUICY

SWEET

segments

BITTER

peel

DIGESTIBLE

GIVE PEOPLE BREAD, NOT A WHEAT FIELD[1]

"Pray that I will proclaim this message as clearly as I should."
Colossians 4:4 (NLT)

We need to make it as easy as possible for the receiver to hear what God wants to communicate. This means working out beforehand exactly what and how much to say.

The acronym *'TMI'* or *'Too much information'* is frequently used these days. This principle can also apply when sharing God's heart with others - it's possible to overshare.

One morning my son wanted a tangerine for his breakfast, so I peeled it and gave it to him and he was happy. If I'd told him to eat the entire unpeeled tangerine, I suspect he wouldn't have been so happy - the juicy sweet flavour would instead have taken on a bitter taste.[2]

God can sometimes communicate to us in personal ways. We need wisdom to know how much of this to share. Sometimes it will be helpful to include the more 'illustrative' way that it came to us (the peel), but other times it could actually be unhelpful, negatively affecting the 'flavour' of the message that God is trying to communicate.

1. When you feel like God is speaking to you, start off by identifying what's at the heart of what God is saying by using only *one* word.
2. Then think about what God is saying as a *simple, single sentence* (like what you'd write in a tweet or on a post-it note.)
3. Then, *if necessary,* let the sentence become sentences, *a paragraph* or several paragraphs.

IDEA – REFLECT

Make sure you don't distract from the main message.

1 I nearly stole my husband's saying and forgot to credit him!

2 Another way of thinking about it is the game *'pass the parcel.'* God gets our attention by revealing the outside 'wrapping paper' to us. But the wrapping paper is not the gift. It's meant to be taken off. If you were asked to unwrap all the many layers yourself, you could get overwhelmed. All you really want is the final layer and gift. We need to help others by removing unnecessary layers so that only the core message remains.

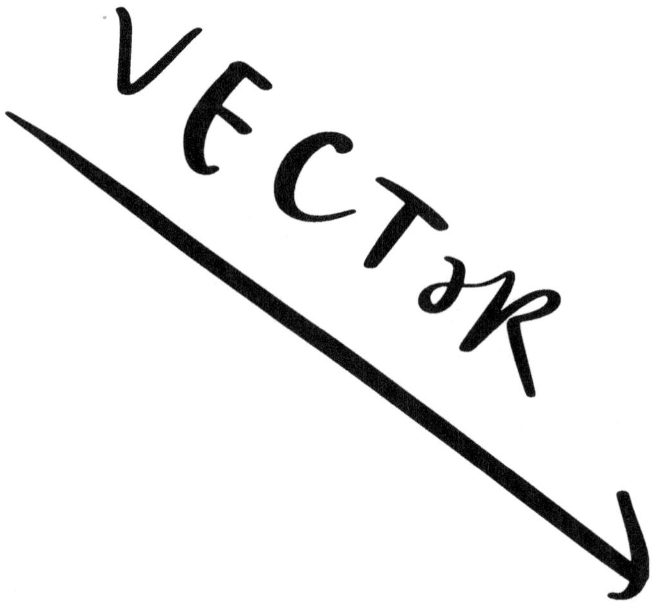

VECTOR

NAME: VECTOR

TO PEEL, OR NOT TO PEEL

TRYING TO WORK OUT HOW & WHAT TO SHARE

I once went to a church meeting and felt God highlight four things to encourage them with.

1. He had created them to be multicultural.
2. He was pleased they had kept their hearts soft during difficult times.
3. Isaiah 58:12 was relevant for them, *"Your people will rebuild the ancient ruins and will raise up the age-old foundations; you will be called Repairer of Broken Walls, Restorer of Streets with Dwellings."*
4. God was going to use them like spiritual garbage collectors in their town.

That's what I felt God wanted me to say. But what was the 'peel' that I chose *not* to share?

Well, the image that originally came into my mind was *Neapolitan ice-cream!* Neapolitan ice-cream has three colours (a *visual* connection – multicultural church). It's often 'soft scoop' (a *word* connection – soft heart). In the UK, *Wall's* ice-cream is the most famous ice-cream brand (a *Scripture* connection – Isaiah 58).

And finally, the spiritual garbage collector part came from a *memory* of a holiday I had in Naples where the garbage collectors were on strike so there was rubbish everywhere.

All of this came from one image, Neapolitan ice-cream. But I never mentioned the image because it would be more distracting than helpful.[1]

On the other hand, here's an example of when I did include the 'peel.' I was praying for someone and a whirlpool vortex came into my mind. As I read up about it, the word *"vector"* kept cropping up. I didn't know whether to share this exact term or simply describe it. But as I prayed, I felt I should share both, although I still didn't know why. The man later told me that his middle name was *"Vector"* – it was his grandfather's name. To him it was a sign that helped him know that God was indeed speaking.[2]

IDEA – ASK

God for wisdom and discernment about what to share.

1 Personally, if someone mentioned ice-cream, all I'd be able to think about would be how I wanted some...

2 It was also helpful feedback for me to learn from.

CHOOSE CAREFULLY

WORD CHOICE

CAREFULLY CHOOSE WHAT WORDS YOU USE

"Make up your mind not to put any stumbling block or obstacle in the way of a brother or sister."
Romans 14:13

When speaking, consider your listener. We don't want to place any kind of barrier or stumbling block in the way that might prevent them from receiving what God wants to say. This includes *what* we say, *how* we say it, and *when* we say it.[1]

When both my boys were very young I went through a time of feeling quite low and frustrated. I'd given up my full-time research for a routine that involved going to the park and toddler groups every day. Although this was my choice, I was still struggling with the change.

I was at a conference one day when a woman approached me. She said she felt God had spoken to her about me and that I was *"depressed."* Knowing what the clinical criteria for depression was, I internally reacted against that word. I was feeling sad and frustrated, but I was not clinically depressed. So I thanked her but was ready to dismiss what she'd said because of the language she'd used.

Before she left, she asked me whether she could pray for me. I agreed. The prayer that courageous woman ended up praying spoke deep into my heart, her words really seemed to come from the heart of God and I was left feeling very blessed.

That evening I reflected upon this experience. I'd almost rejected everything she'd shared simply because of a single word. What she'd probably sensed was a sadness (correct), but she'd labelled that as 'depressed' (unhelpful for me). She'd heard from God correctly, but translated it in a way that had been a *barrier* for me.

IDEA – REMEMBER

Communicate clearly and simply, without confusing words or spiritual jargon.

1 Sometimes it's helpful to ask, *"would a child, or someone who's not a Christian, understand what I'm saying?"* It can highlight what kind of language to use or avoid.

DON'T UNDERESTIMATE

QUALITY VS. QUANTITY

WHAT YOU SAY > HOW MUCH YOU SAY

"'Is not my word like fire,' declares the Lord, 'and like a hammer that breaks a rock in pieces?'"
Jeremiah 23:29

Now that we've clarified that love and godly authenticity are important, let's now talk about length. Does 'word count' matter?

Yes... be short!

What we're aiming for is *quality* rather than quantity, purity over waffle! Our words don't need to be lengthy in order to be meaningful. If they're from God, they will be powerful. Even if you feel like God has just given you one single word, don't add to it! Only speak the words God gives you; adding anything may dilute what He's saying.

I was once part of a prayer team. My prayer partner was experienced and could talk for a long time about what He felt God was saying. In contrast, what I shared was short and simple.

A young man came for prayer and as my partner began to speak I started to feel quite disheartened about my short verbal offerings! After my prayer partner had spoken at great length, it was my turn. All I had in my mind was a picture of a jack-in-a-box. I felt this was about things feeling tight, but that pressure would soon come to an end and the tension would go. It took me 40 seconds to share. The interesting thing was that although the person we'd been praying for had previously been rather stoic when my partner had prayed, when I gave this tiny word, he started to cry. He explained that he'd been under incredible pressure and to know it wasn't going to last forever brought great relief.

IDEA – REFLECT

Don't underestimate the power of short, simple words.

If they're from God, they will be powerful.

I FEEL
GOD
SAYING...

SHARE WITH HUMILITY

DON'T SAY, "THUS SAYS THE LORD...!"

"Do nothing out of selfish ambition or vain conceit. Rather, in humility value others above yourselves, not looking to your own interests but each of you to the interests of the others."
Philippians 2:3-4

Always share what you're saying with *humility.*

In his book, *"Do what Jesus did"*[1] Robby Dawkins advises that no matter how clearly you hear God speaking or how strongly you sense what you have is from Him, we should always phrase our words in such a way that the responsibility is on us.

"I think God is saying... I feel God is showing me... I sense God is telling you..."

This keeps things subjective and creates a safer environment for people. Every word we feel is from God always remains subject to judgment by others to decide for themselves whether they think it's from God or not.

I have a friend who uses the following phrase:
"Hi, I'm a Christian and sometimes I feel that God speaks to me, but I'm still learning! I think He may be sharing something with me for you. Would you mind if I told you it so you can decide whether you feel as though it's from God or not?"[2]

I found this helpful. You'll notice how he doesn't say, *"Thus sayeth the Lord..."* And how he humbly asks permission to speak instead of assuming that they'll want to hear what he has to say.

Share what you feel God is saying with humility and without manipulation.

IDEA – THINK

How would you phrase something you felt was from God?

1 This is one of my favourite books - it's full of amazing stories. I highly recommend it.

2 Thanks for this helpful advice, Paul Maconochie.

FOCUS ON

HOPE

FOCUS ON HOPE

GOD'S MESSAGES SHOULD ALWAYS BRING LIFE

"'For I know the plans I have for you,' declares the Lord 'plans to prosper you and not to harm you, plans to give you hope and a future.'"
Jeremiah 29:11

A while ago something odd happened when I flushed our upstairs toilet. I heard what sounded like a bucket of water being dumped from above into our garden. At first I thought nothing of it, but soon realised that it was happening *every time* I flushed the loo, so I went outside to investigate.

There, up high, I could see a problem.

The outside waste piping that flushed the contents of the loo into the sewage drain had come apart. As a result, each time the toilet had been flushed, the contents had spilt into the garden. This was not a pleasant sight![1]

Our role as people who can hear God's heart for others is not to focus on the negative, but rather to bring solutions from God's way of seeing things. We're not meant to expose the mess in people's lives, we're supposed to help clean it up.

Jesus was never motivated to use the revelation He received to shame anyone;[2] it was always used to build them up and bring them into their God-given identity.

God's words should always leave us feeling full of hope and cause us to want to run towards Jesus rather than to hide from Him.

IDEA – THINK

Dig for the gold, not the dirt!

God restores, redeems and renews.

1 No wonder my sunflower plant had suddenly died... although, perhaps it should have flourished!

2 See John 4, the story of the Samaritan woman at the well, as an example of this.

LEAVE THE GAPS ______.

LEAVE GAPS BLANK

OUR KNOWLEDGE WILL ALWAYS BE LIMITED

"We know in part and prophesy in part."
1 Corinthians 13:9

One morning our whole neighbourhood was awakened by the sound of side-splitting laughter - you know the kind when you try to talk but instead a high-pitched squeak comes out. It was my two boys. They were in such hysterics they couldn't contain themselves, although I had no idea why.

So I asked them to fill me in [cue more pig-snort laughter].

Once he'd managed to catch his breath, my youngest eventually piped up: *"Last night I caught Daddy watching My Little Pony!"* And with that they were off again, doubled over by the memory of their father watching a little girl's TV programme.

Now you need to know something – that's absolutely true. But it's not the whole story. Daniel had been watching a documentary about toys and merchandise. It reviewed the ones that had flopped and the ones that had staggered everyone by their unprecedented success and longevity. And yes, a review of My Little Pony was shown, just as my kids walked in.

Here's the point – context is important.

Whenever we hear from God, both for ourselves and for others, we need to remember that we will only be getting part of the whole picture and it's important that we don't try to fill in the blanks with our own guesses and assumptions.[1]

IDEA – REMEMBER

When God shows you something, it's only a small part of a bigger picture. There will always be things we don't know.

1 Like predictive text / auto-correct when it epically fails (and you realise too late...)

FAITHFUL NOT FAKE

STAY TRUE TO GOD'S WORDS

"I will put my words in his mouth. He will tell them everything I command him."
Deuteronomy 18:18

For one of my birthdays I really wanted a tan leather jacket. I found one which I liked that was pretty expensive but I thought that it was worth combining my birthday money together for it. When the day arrived I knew it had been worth the wait - it was so buttery soft I couldn't help stroking it. It really was a craftsman's work of art with all its fine, hand stitching.

Then I went to the garage. I got out some 40 grit sandpaper and walnut shoe polish and proceeded to vigorously scrape the elbows and edges of my brand new jacket. Then I got a handful of polish and worked it into the roughed up areas.

What on *earth* was I doing?

I wanted the jacket to look 'vintage' and worn in and had seen a hack on YouTube about how to do this. So I was just going for it - making my brand new leather jacket look old.[1]

Another way of describing what I was doing is 'faking it'.

Sometimes we might be tempted to fake or knowingly modify what we're sharing with others. We might feel that it's not enough, it's too short or it's too weak sounding. But it's really important that we are faithful with what we have.

IDEA – REMEMBER

Resist the temptation to exaggerate, fabricate or manipulate what you feel God is saying to you.

1 It 'kind of' worked. I don't think it would pass off as genuine vintage though...

SPEAK WHAT GOD SAYS

DON'T SPEAK WORDS TO KEEP PEOPLE HAPPY

GOD'S APPROVAL

BE LOYAL TO GOD, NOT MAN

"As surely as the Lord lives, I can tell him only what the Lord tells me."
1 Kings 22:14

In 1 Kings 22 we read how Micaiah the prophet was asked to share what He felt God was saying to King Ahab. King Ahab wasn't a fan of Micaiah, because he refused to prophesy good things to Ahab just to keep him happy. There was lots of pressure and manipulation for Micaiah to tell King Ahab what He wanted to hear.

"Look, the other prophets without exception are predicting success for the king. Let your word agree with theirs, and speak favourably."[1]

But Micaiah refused to be forced into speaking any words that weren't from the Lord.

"As surely as the Lord lives, I can tell him only what the Lord tells me."

It's so important that we are people God can trust and who are faithful with His words as we represent Him to others.

God trusts those who won't be manipulated - who act for God's approval, not man's.

Paul says it well in his letter to the Galatians. *"Am I now trying to win the approval of human beings, or of God? Or am I trying to please people? If I were still trying to please people, I would not be a servant of Christ."*[2]

Live and speak for God's approval.
Only say what He says.

IDEA - READ

Numbers 22:38

"But I can't say whatever I please. I must speak only what God puts in my mouth."

1 See 1 Kings 22:13
2 Look at Galatians 1:10

SEEMS
SOMETIMES BEING OBEDIENT
BONKERS

BONKERS OBEDIENCE

OBEY EVEN WHEN IT DOESN'T MAKE SENSE

"Do whatever He tells you."
John 2:5

"It's bonkers!"

I was at a church service one Sunday when a friend came up to me to return a children's science kit that I had left behind at her house. It was a kit that enabled you to make odd, cuboid shaped bubbles using straws. The kit was called *Bonkers Bubbles.*

As she gave it to me I felt a nudge in my spirit that seemed to imply that I'd be needing that kit later. I had no idea why, because I was at church after all. What use was a *Bonkers Bubbles* kit at church?

Towards the end of the service we were encouraged to pray for people. I felt I should pray for one particular man and as I did, I felt I should go and get my *Bonkers Bubbles* kit. Not knowing anything that the man was going through, I found myself saying something like, *"I feel God wants to say something through this kit. He is changing and reshaping structures around you and at times things are going to seem bonkers. But He is in control and He is doing a new thing."*

What came out of my mouth made no sense to me *whatsoever,* but I shared it anyway because I felt God was encouraging me to do so.

The man later fed back to me that his company had indeed been going through a time of all kinds of unusual changes and restructuring and that during the weeks that followed he'd found himself repeatedly saying, *"this is just bonkers!"* What made no sense to me at the time made a lot of sense to him that month.

Our role is to be faithful and obedient and to not second-guess the relevance of what God gives us to share. If we are hearing correctly, God will clarify the significance to the person.

IDEA – READ

Deuteronomy 13:3–4

"Worship the Lord your God, fear him, obey his commands, listen to what he says, serve him, and be loyal to him."

WHEN TO SPEAK

WORKING OUT TIMING

So far we've considered the fact that when we feel like God is speaking to us for another person, that we need to ask Him about exactly *how* and *what* He wants us to share. This is because we want to make sure that we communicate His message as clearly and as lovingly as possible.

The next question to ask God is: *When* should you share His message? Timing is very important.

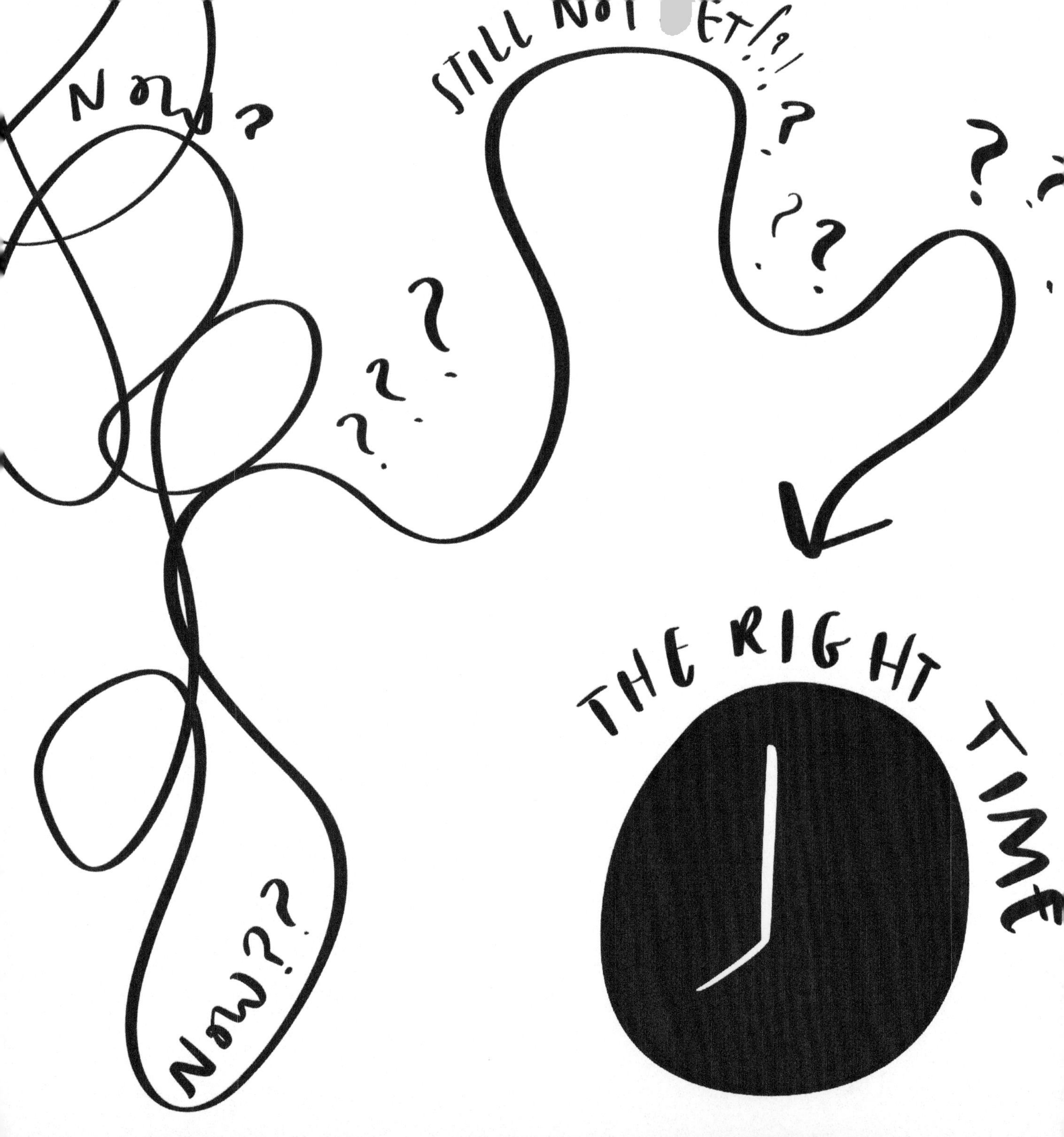
NOW?
STILL NOT
NOW??
THE RIGHT TIME

TIMING IS KEY

WHEN YOU SPEAK IS REALLY IMPORTANT

"The right thing at the wrong time is the wrong thing."
Daniel Goodman

You press the doorbell with great eagerness and anticipation. Your stomach is growling and you've purposely not eaten much throughout the day so you'll have extra space for tonight. You wonder what they're going to be cooking and start to salivate at the prospect of what's for dinner. You hear the footsteps of the host arriving to let you in and you prepare your best 'greetings' face.The door opens and a blanket of warm air wraps around you from inside.

But wait, something's wrong.

Across your host's face, just for a fleeting second, an odd expression flickers. You pay no real attention to that minor detail as you deliver a hearty hug and step right into their hallway making yourself instantly at home as you take off your coat and scarf in one swift movement. But something is amiss.

"We were expecting you yesterday," your host says quietly.

You look at your watch to check the date and suddenly a wave of cold blood courses through your body. You've got the wrong day. Not only did you arrive on the wrong day, you arrived the day *after* you were supposed to be there. That means that yesterday they had carefully prepared your meal and the pudding of all puddings. Yesterday. You gasp in utter horror at your mistake, not knowing what to do...[1]

Timing matters.

IDEA - READ

Proverbs 19:2

"Even zeal is no good without knowledge, and he who hurries his footsteps misses the mark."[2]

1 I would like to say this story was fabricated for the sake of illustrating a point... but I can't.

2 This is from the Berean Study Bible (BSB) Version

GOD'S WORDS
GO!
GO!
GO!
GO!
WAIT...
WAIT...
WAIT...
WAIT...
WAIT...
PASS ON

INCUBATION

LET GOD'S WORDS GROW & MATURE IN YOUR HEART

"Mary treasured up all these things and pondered them in her heart."
Luke 2:19

What do you do when you're handed a hot potato? You don't want your fingers to burn so you pass it on as soon as possible. Right? Or do you? When I first started to realise that God was actually speaking to *me,* I got so excited that I treated what He said like a hot potato. I thought I had to share it as soon as possible the moment I recognised it was from God. I felt like if there was any delay in sharing what God had spoken to me about, then I was somehow being unfaithful and disobedient. But that's just not true. Yes, it really *is* exciting when we realise that the God of all creation is speaking to us, there's no doubt about that! But we don't need to pass on what He says as soon as we hear it.

One of the reasons why waiting is wise is that sometimes God wants to 'grow' what He's sharing with you, just as a seed grows over time or as a cake needs time to bake in an oven.

I mentioned previously how God often invites us to begin a conversation with Him, which often involves us asking questions. Sometimes this kind of conversation may take months or even years! In order for a baby to be born healthy and strong, it's important that it's not born too early. Sometimes God's words are like that. We may feel like we are carrying them for months, but we need to allow God the time to develop and mature them fully in our hearts. Once we recognise that the conversation has stopped, then we can think about sharing what God has been saying all that time.

It takes practice, patience and wisdom to work out when to speak and when to stay silent.

When God speaks, don't rush ahead.

IDEA - READ

James 1:19

"Let every person be quick to hear, slow to speak."

WHEN
TO
SHARE
OR
TO KEEP
HOLD

JUMP-THE-GUN JOSEPH

BE SLOW TO SPEAK

"Do not be quick with your mouth"
Ecclesiastes 5:2

In Genesis 37 we read a story about a man called Joseph. His brothers didn't like him because he was the golden child, favoured by his father. Joseph then had two dreams about his brothers bowing down to him[1] and for some reason Joseph decided it would be a good idea to tell his brothers about it! They didn't respond well, *"and when he told it to his brothers, they hated him all the more."*[2] The next thing we find out, the brothers are plotting to kill Joseph.

I wonder if Joseph asked God whether he was allowed to share that dream or whether he rushed ahead and did it anyway, carried away in excitement about the fact that God was speaking to him about his future. It doesn't seem like a wise thing to do – to know that your brothers are struggling with how highly favoured you are and then essentially rubbing it in their faces by saying one day they are going to bow down to him!

Being able to work out *when to share* God's heart and *when to keep hold of* it is a discipline that is important to grow in. Thankfully, just as in Joseph's case, even if we get it wrong God gives us great grace and is very patient with us. He is always able to fix our messes!

"Set a guard over my mouth, Lord; keep watch over the door of my lips."
(Psalm 141:3)

IDEA – THINK

Have you ever made a mistake by speaking too quickly?

1 Have a look at Genesis 37:6-9, but keep your Bible open because there's another reference coming up.

2 Genesis 37:5

GOD NUDGES

GOD NUDGES

WAIT UNTIL GOD SAYS "GO!"

"A time to be silent and a time to speak"
Ecclesiastes 3:7

I have a wise friend called Rosemary and she is very good at waiting. She's taught me a lot about not rushing in with the things that God is speaking to me about. She once told me that she waits for what she calls, *"God nudges",* or key-word triggers to let her know when it's the right time to share something. For example, if she felt like God was speaking to us as a church about being like a windmill and someone in the service mentioned something windmill-related, then she'd know that it was God's way of showing her that the time was right.

A fantastic example of this was when I'd first written a draft of this book. Having seen a copy for the first time, Rosemary sent me an email in which she said:

"I had no idea you were writing a book, but on 28th July last year I had been praying and wrote in my journal, 'Picture of Anna Goodman with her book published! God is giving her a story to write. She is still in the first chapters. There is so much more to come.' "

That was so encouraging for me to receive. God had told Rosemary He was preparing me to write a book before I knew anything about it! What really struck me was that if Rosemary had told me immediately about what God had said to her, it would have had a very different impact. I probably would have felt very overwhelmed by the idea because of what was already going on in my life. Rather than the book-writing journey happening naturally like it did later, it would have instead come from a place of pressure.

Rosemary waited for the right time to speak and so must we.

IDEA – THINK

Wait for God's 'green light' before you 'go'!

CAN I SHARE THIS?

PERMISSION

DON'T ASSUME EVERYTHING IS FOR SHARING

"I no longer call you servants, because a servant does not know his master's business. Instead, I have called you friends"
John 15:15

My husband helps lead the church that we go to and, as a result of this, he is often told lots of very personal things. We have a rule that unless explicitly stated otherwise, I should consider that everything he shares with me is confidential. That's our default position.

Sometimes God just wants to share things with us with no need to pass it on any further. He just wants you to pray about it. Amazing as it is, God considers us to be His friends. It's therefore important we don't assume that everything is for passing on and that we only open our mouths once He's actually given us *permission* to share.

I want to close this chapter with one last comment. I've highlighted the importance of timing - knowing *when* to share (*if* indeed we are to share). The final stage is working out when to *stop.*

Have you ever over-baked or over-cooked something so that it became too dry, over-cooked or stodgy?! Sometimes we can over-analyse, over-interpret or over-talk what we've been entrusted with. If we do this, it stops being fresh.

Don't over-bake your bread. Give what God's given you, then stop!

IDEA - THINK

Have you ever shared something that you later realised was confidential?

God confides in us, His friends. Not everything He says is to be spoken out loud.

Sometimes we should just pray.

THE AFTER PARTY

WHAT TO DO ONCE YOU'VE SHARED SOMETHING

Once you've taken that courageous step of sharing what you feel God is saying with another person, then what do you do? This is what we're going to talk about next.

Then in the following chapter, I'll talk about some of the things that you can advise them to do.

TUNING FORKS

GETTING FEEDBACK WILL HELP YOU GROW

"As iron sharpens iron, so one person sharpens another."
Proverbs 27:17

In an orchestra, there are many instruments. Each different instrument is capable of producing its own range of unique and beautiful notes. However, in order for it to do that, the person playing the instrument needs to learn how to play it in the correct way, which takes time and practice. They also need to make sure that their instrument is in tune.

Getting feedback is like a tuning fork. It helps us know when we need to make adjustments in how we listen, understand and share God's voice. If you don't know you're playing a 'wrong note', you'll keep playing it.

Therefore, once you've shared something you feel is from God, get honest feedback as soon as possible whilst the message is still fresh and the tune still lingers in the air. This will help you *learn, discern* and *mature.*

If no-one offers you feedback, intentionally seek it out.[1] We must always be teachable and willing to be corrected, not only by God but also by people that God puts in our lives. Having a church family who are prepared to speak honestly to you will help keep you safe and grounded in truth and will help you grow.[2]

Feedback is important because we're *accountable* for the words we speak and the mistakes we make. If we've got it wrong, we need to carefully *apologise* and clean up carefully to ensure that no-one gets hurt and that God's reputation and heart isn't left misrepresented.

IDEA – THINK

Who in your life could give you honest feedback?

---

1 This sometimes requires giving people explicit permission to speak into our lives in an honest way.

2 I have someone who has really helped me grow in this area. He's very loving in how he gives me feedback but he does challenge me where necessary when I haven't quite got it right or if I could have been clearer. He's one of my 'tuning forks.' I'm so grateful for his input because it has helped me grow.

SPECIFIC
LOVING

GIVING FEEDBACK

HELPING OTHERS TO GROW

"Speaking the truth in love, we will grow to become in every respect the mature body of him who is the head, that is, Christ."
Ephesians 4:15

When someone has shared something with you, try to give *them* feedback as soon as appropriate. It will help them grow on their journey. The best kind of feedback is *specific* and *loving.*

For example, you could say:
"The bit that you said about having a heart for the homeless really ties in with what I feel God has been speaking to me about recently. In fact, you won't know this, but I've recently done some research about setting up a charity to help those who are struggling to find a home.

"However, the bit you said about the parachute didn't really connect with me. Do you have any more detail that might help bring clarity? Perhaps it's something that will make more sense over time!"

I once shared something with someone and got the interpretation totally wrong. I didn't know this person, but she fed back through a friend that what I had shared made absolutely no sense to her![1] I offered to meet up to emphasise that I was still learning and to get some specific feedback so I could identify where I'd gone wrong. I'm so glad I did this, even though it wasn't an easy conversation to have at first.

I described the initial picture I'd had in my mind and went on to say how I'd interpreted it. As we talked it became apparent that I'd jumped to conclusions and made assumptions. She then said that she felt she knew what God had been trying to say from my initial picture. I'm so glad I took the time to speak with her because she ended up being really touched by God's (actual) message and I learnt some valuable lessons (which was mainly, don't make *assumptions* or *jump to conclusions).*

IDEA – THINK

What's the most helpful feedback you've ever been given?

1 Ow!

THAT'S HOW
I MADE HIM
FEEL

WHAT HAVE THEY HEARD?

HOW HAS WHAT YOU'VE SAID BEEN UNDERSTOOD?

Have you ever looked at yourself in a funfair mirror, the kind that has curves in it? Your reflection looks like you, but it's distorted, isn't it? Whether we're aware of it or not, everyone has filters that they hear and see things through; areas of sensitivity and vulnerability that we won't always be aware of. Therefore, sometimes what we say and what is heard is different.

I learnt a hard lesson recently. I was being interviewed and as part of my answer I said God always wants to show us things from His perspective - to bring solutions to problems and hope to hopeless situations.

A young man thanked me for my comment. He continued, *"A few years ago, you were at my youth group teaching us how to hear God's voice. At one point, you told me off for what I said. That hurt me, but now I understand what you were trying to say."*

I was shocked and embarrassed. As much as I tried, I simply couldn't remember reprimanding this man. So I asked him to elaborate. He described how he'd 'seen' a person wearing chains and how I'd told him what he'd shared was too negative. He said he now understood what I'd been trying to say, which was to ask God for His positive perspective.

I still can't believe I actually told him off, but that's not the point. The point is that in that moment I made him *feel* told off.[1]

Some advice I've been given is to ask the person you're talking to, *"What do you think I've said to you?"* This then helps you to know if you need to clarify any area of misunderstanding. It also allows room for you to apologise if you haven't come across in a way that has left someone feeling full of love, life and hope.[2]

IDEA – DO

Give people a chance to reflect back what they've heard.

1 *"I've learned that people will forget what you said, people will forget what you did, but people will never forget how you made them feel."* Maya Angelou

2 That's why I think it's good to always have a witness and to make a recording (audio or written) of what you share with others.

OUR VALUE...
HOW GOD SEES
WHAT GOD SAYS

UNCONDITIONAL ACCEPTANCE

YOUR WORTH IS NOT DETERMINED BY YOUR PERFORMANCE

"But you are a chosen people, a royal priesthood, a holy nation, God's special possession, that you may declare the praises of him who called you out of darkness into his wonderful light."
1 Peter 2:9

We live in a time where people are no longer thought to have high or low self-esteem, but rather, *"contingent self-esteem".*[1] This is the belief that worth must be earned. Direct or indirect approval of others is therefore needed in order to determine how someone values themselves.

Henri Nouwen describes *three big lies:*

1. I am what I have
2. I am what I do
3. I am what other people say about me.

These *are* lies and are *not* built on God's truth.

Sometimes when we share God's heart with others, we will get different responses. Sometimes people won't respond at all, other times their feedback might be difficult to hear and sometimes people's reactions could be so positive we might be tempted to get puffed up with pride: *"Check me out, I can hear God so well!"*

Whatever the feedback, we must remember that first and foremost we are God's precious children and our value and worth comes from Him and Him alone.[2]

IDEA – REFLECT

Our self-esteem should always be built on what God says about us and not on our performance, good or bad.

---

1 Jordan C.H., Zeigler-Hill V. (2018) Contingent Self-Esteem. In: Zeigler-Hill V., Shackelford T. (eds) Encyclopedia of Personality and Individual Differences. Springer, Cham

2 A filthy bank note is worth as much as a clean one. Its value comes from the Government's guarantee, not from its physical condition.

GOD'S LOVE
GOD'S
MESSAGE

GRACIOUS GOD

IN OUR WEAKNESS, HE IS STRONG

"The Spirit helps us in our weakness."
Romans 8:26

The other day, my eldest came up to me with such a sweet and almost shy smile on his face.

"If you're thinking you still need to clean up the kitchen - you don't need to, I've done it for you."

He explained that he'd seen me working so hard and had wanted to do something for me. So he'd washed up the plates that were in the sink along with the butter dish and had put away all the other little piles that had formed on the counter top - all out of a heart of wanting to help me.

All the plates and the butter dish needed to be rewashed and certain things had been rehomed in the wrong place, but that didn't matter at all to me. All that mattered was that my son had thought about me and had wanted to help.

Moments like these help me when I get things wrong. If my heart has been right, then I know that God still delights in the fact that I tried my best. Even in my weakness the Holy Spirit can still be at work!

If your primary goal is to communicate God's love when sharing something for someone, but for some reason you didn't quite get it right, you have not failed. Love is always the main goal and love never fails.[1]

IDEA - READ

2 Corinthians 12:9

"My grace is sufficient for you, for my power is made perfect in weakness."

1 See 1 Corinthians 13:8. Slightly-relevant-and-funny story: I once accidentally sent my ex-boss a message that I meant to send to my husband who was away on a business trip. I wrote, *"I love you and I miss you and I love you and I miss you."* I was so embarrassed when I initially found out my mistake, but my boss found it hilarious - he knew it had been sent in error. We laughed a lot about it afterwards. Love never fails.

BABOONS?!?

GREAT EXPECTATIONS

GOD'S WAYS ARE BETTER THAN OURS

"'For my thoughts are not your thoughts, neither are your ways my ways,' declares the Lord."
Isaiah 55:8-9

Once I asked my husband to buy some shoes for my youngest because he'd outgrown his last pair. What I had in mind were some versatile shoes that would blend into whatever he was wearing. I'm almost completely sure that those were my instructions – *subtle, everyday shoes.*

What I got was not that.

My husband came back later with a mischievous look on his face – a grin that told me I needed to be prepared for the worst. And I was right. Because out of the bag came a box. And inside the box were the shoes. Baboon shoes.

If you've ever seen the *'Lion King'* before, think *'Rafiki'* – you know, the monkey with bright blue and red features and the wild, crazy eyes? Yes, now think about his mad baboon face on my three-year-old's shoes. They even had a floppy mane that could be flipped and flapped if you so desired (which my husband clearly did).

What I had *needed* and what my husband thought my son actually *wanted* were two very, very different things. I got what I asked for – shoes. I just didn't get the *kind* of shoes I was *expecting* and *hoping* for. But do you know what? Those shoes were my son's favourite shoes. He loved them so much and they brought him so much joy and everyone who saw them chuckled. They were shoes that brought happiness.

This is how it sometimes works with God. We hope and pray for a particular thing. But God, who is Sovereign and knows best, gives us something else. It's kind of what we asked for, but it's not what we would have necessarily chosen if it was up to us ourselves.

IDEA – REFLECT

Has God ever acted in a very different way than you expected?

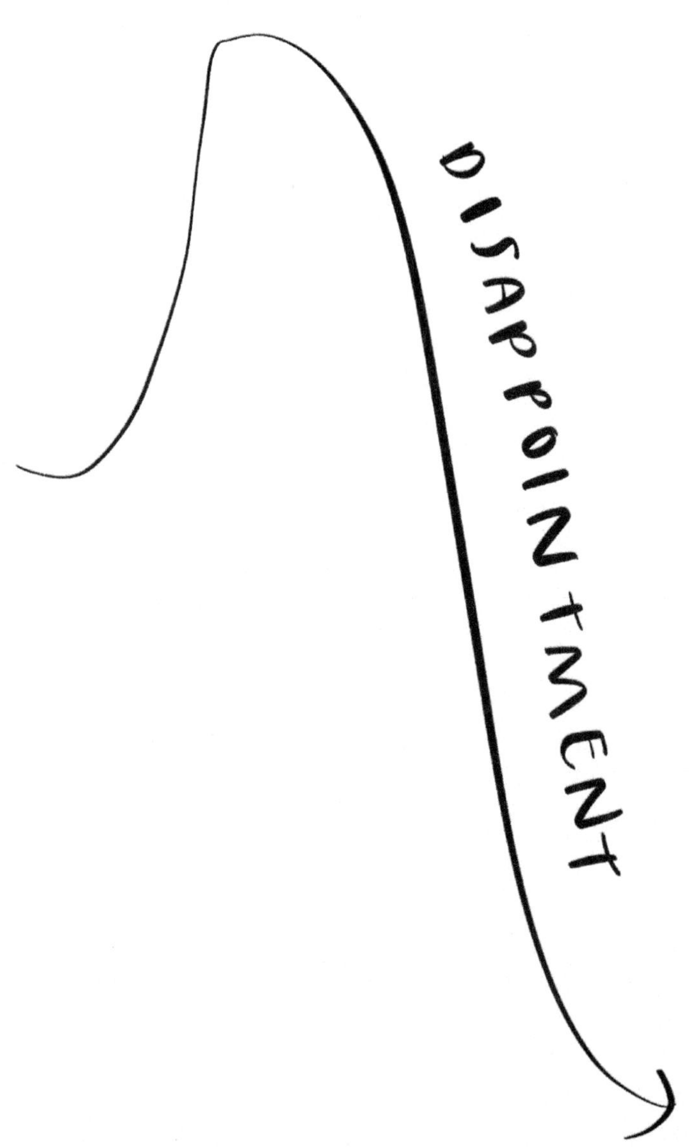
DISAPPOINTMENT

DISAPPOINTMENT

GOD'S AGENDA ISN'T ALWAYS THE SAME AS OURS

"Today, if you hear his voice, do not harden your hearts"
Psalm 95:7-8

"I have no idea what you're talking about," he said.

I was gutted.

Recently at a Christian gathering I shared something I thought was from God for someone and they totally rejected what I said to them. It was a bit painful to hear, particularly because other people witnessed me getting it completely wrong, but I just asked God to help me learn from my mistake and keep my heart soft.

Almost a year later, the same man came and found me and apologised. He said that what I had shared had been accurate, but at the time he didn't want to accept it because he had come to that gathering wanting God to speak to him about *something else.* He didn't like the fact that God decided to speak to him about another matter and therefore had rejected it at the time.

People (including ourselves, sometimes) will want God to speak about certain things and often God won't actually choose to talk about that thing. We can have expectations that might not be met. God's agenda and priorities aren't always the same as ours and sometimes this can bring disappointment.

When God is not talking about the things we want Him to be talking about, we have a choice. We can either ignore what God is saying or we can re-adjust ourselves to have ears to hear what God *actually* thinks is important for us to know or hear in that moment in time.

What God is focused on is really what we need to be focused on. His perspective needs to be our perspective. His priorities need to be our priorities.

IDEA – CONSIDER

Sometimes being faithful to God will mean we disappoint people.

Keep being faithful anyway!

GOD
CARRIERS OF GOD'S WORD
BE HUMBLE
RECIPIENT

THE DONKEY

GIVE GOD ALL THE GLORY

"They brought the donkey and the colt and placed their cloaks on them for Jesus to sit on. A very large crowd spread their cloaks on the road, while others cut branches from the trees and spread them on the road. The crowds that went ahead of him and those that followed shouted,'Hosanna to the Son of David!'"
Matthew 21:7-9

At the beginning of this book, I wrote about Moses. He talked with God face-to-face and He was also the most humble man on the face of the earth.[1] I want to end this chapter by talking again about the importance of humility. Sometimes, you might be tempted to think: *"Check me out! I can hear God so well!"* But pride has no place before God.

I found what Reinhard Hirtler says about the verse we just read really helpful.

"How stupid would it have been if the donkey had boasted to all the other donkeys when he got back to his stall that evening about how people celebrated him! They celebrated the Lord; he was only the one carrying Him. In the same way, we only carry the gift or the anointing. We are never the source; the Lord is."[2]

If you want to keep hearing from God, keep your heart humble.

IDEA – READ

James 4:6

"God opposes the proud but shows favour to the humble."

1 Numbers 12:3 tells us this.

2 Hirtler, R. (2014) Balancing the prophetic. Equipping the Church in the Prophetic Ministry.

RESPONSIBILITY

WEIGH, PRAY, TREASURE + OBEY

Our topic for this chapter is 'taking responsibility'.

It's not your responsibility whether a person accepts what you have shared with them. They need to personally take responsibility and decide whether they think it's from God or not.

1. *Weigh* – weigh or test what has been shared and decide whether it's God or not.
2. *Pray* – say *"thank you"* and ask God whether there's anything else He wants to say.
3. *Treasure* – protect and look after what God has said. Keep reminding yourself of His promises.
4. *Obey* – we need to be obedient and take action, where necessary.

"The Lord our God has secrets known to no one. We are not accountable for them, but we and our children are accountable forever for all that he has revealed to us, so that we may obey all the terms of these instructions."

Deuteronomy 29:29 (NLT)

WHAT WE HEARD

CONFIRMATION

WISE COUNSEL

Holy Spirit

SCRIPTURE

TEST & WEIGH

WORKING OUT WHETHER SOMETHING IS FROM GOD

"Do not quench the Spirit. Do not treat prophecies with contempt but test them all; hold on to what is good."
1 Thessalonians 5:21

There are several things we can do to help us test whether what we're hearing is from God or not.

1. *Scripture* – Does it agree with what Scripture teaches? God won't contradict Himself.

2. *Holy Spirit* – If I were to drop a rubber ball on a hard floor it would bounce, wouldn't it? However, if I were to drop a bean bag on the same floor, it would just go 'thud,' no bounce at all. I find that when something is from God, the Holy Spirit responds a bit like a bounce in my heart, as though He's saying: *"Yes, that's right! That's from me!"* If it isn't from God then it just feels like an empty thud in my heart.[1]

3. *Wise counsel* – Ask trusted, wise and Godly people what they think.

4. *Confirmation* – Does what I'm hearing align with what God has *already* said? When God speaks He's often bringing confirmation.

Do bear in mind that *some* parts might be from God, but other parts might not be. If so, don't dismiss it all – chew the meat, spit out the bones! If you're not sure or clear about anything that has been shared, put it to the side for now.[2]

IDEA - READ

1 Corinthians 14:29

"Two or three prophets should speak, and the others should weigh carefully what is said."

1 I call this my *"Bouncy ball or bean bag test".* Yes, I actually gave it a name.

2 Do write it down and revisit it later though – sometimes what makes no sense at the time will become clearer later on. (*"Jesus replied, "You do not realise now what I am doing, but later you will understand"."* John 13:7)

God's words are valuable

TREASURE & OBEY

VALUE GOD'S WORDS & TAKE ACTION IF NECESSARY

"Write the vision; make it plain on tablets, so he may run who reads it."
Habakkuk 2:2

We live in a consumer culture. We want things passionately in the moment, but tomorrow we're bored and disinterested.

But God's words aren't cheap.

I have a box of precious items, objects that are priceless to me. But that box is stored up on top of my cupboard and every day it collects dust.

Psalm 119:11 says, *"I have stored up your word in my heart".* When God speaks to us, we need to treat His words as precious. They're not supposed to be written in a special book and forgotten about. They're supposed to be treated with the care and attention they deserve. I find the following process helpful:

1. *Write* down what God has said
2. *Colour* it in!

a) Highlight in *green* the parts that speak about what God says about you. This is *truth* to line up with. *Thank* Him for His words!

b) Highlight in *red* the parts that speak about what God says He's going to do. These are promises to *pray* back to God. *"Do it, Lord!"*

c) Highlight in *yellow*[1] the things you're encouraged to do. This is truth to act upon. Be obedient. *Take action* if necessary.[2]

IDEA – REFLECT

Have you got any words that you feel are from God?

Why not apply the above process to them?

1 If you don't like these colours, feel free to pick your own! Thank you, Mike Bollinger, for sharing this helpful process.

2 *"But be doers of the word, and not hearers only, deceiving yourselves. For if anyone is a hearer of the word and not a doer, he is like a man observing his natural face in a mirror; for he observes himself, goes away, and immediately forgets what kind of man he was."* James 1:22-24

W A I T . . .

IF IT SEEMS SLOW, WAIT

GOD'S TIMING IS DIFFERENT TO OURS

"For still the vision awaits its appointed time; it hastens to the end – it will not lie. If it seems slow, wait for it; it will surely come; it will not delay."
Habakkuk 2:3

When children are very young, they don't really have a concept of time. My youngest would say things like, *"You know that place we went to yesterday?"* And for him *"yesterday"* meant any time and experience that that had already happened, not literally yesterday. The same applied for the word *"tomorrow". "I'm looking forward to going to Big Grandad's house tomorrow."* To him, *"tomorrow"* simply meant something that was going to happen in the future.

When we hear and see the things that God is showing us, we won't always know the exact timing involved. We may expect something to be imminent when in fact it's going to happen in 15 years time.[1]

Don't give up or dismiss what God has said because something hasn't happened immediately. Our timing is not like His.

At one point in my life, I'd been praying hard about three things we needed breakthrough for. I remember feeling frustrated because nothing seemed to be changing.

Then one day a catapult came into my mind. I felt God say that although we were in a time of tension and waiting, it was necessary. But all three things we'd been praying for would happen at the same time, just like a catapult being fired. And that's exactly what happened. All three things took place on exactly the same day in a way that *only* God could have co-ordinated. God's timing is perfect and worth waiting for.

IDEA – READ

2 Peter 3:8

With the Lord a day is like a thousand years, and a thousand years are like a day."

1 And actually for a God who has existed for all eternity, 15 years of time could be seen as 'imminent' from His perspective!

GOLDEN
MARMALADE

GOLDEN MARMALADE

A STORY

"The Lord is trustworthy in all he promises and faithful in all he does."
Psalm 145:13

I'd like to give an example that summarises many of the points I've been trying to make.

I once was praying for a friend and a picture of a jar came into my mind. As I focused on it, the security bubble on the top popped up as though the jar had just been opened *(the invitation revelation).*

So, I asked God what this meant *(gaining understanding through conversation).* I then got a sense that the jar represented a job opportunity that was going to open up *(the interpretation).*

I then asked God what the jar contained *(further questions for more detail).* The words *'Golden Marmalade'* came into my mind. Almost immediately I then found myself connecting marmalade to Paddington Bear[1] *(an association).* My flow of thought then focused on two things: 1) Paddington's suitcase (i.e. travelling) and 2) the association with London's Paddington Railway Station.

I therefore felt God was saying he was going to give this man a job that was going to involve some commuting, possibly via London[2] *(interpretation).*

When I asked God if there was anything else relevant, I remembered how jars of marmalade say *"consume within x amount of days".* I therefore felt that this opportunity was not a long-term solution, but rather a stepping stone, possibly a short-term contract *(further interpretation).*

The family weighed it and prayed about it *(weighing).* Later my friend told me that he'd just got a short-term contract that involved travelling through Paddington Station in London *(feedback and fulfilment of God's words).*

1 A fictional character in children's literature. He was discovered in Paddington Station, London, by the Brown family who adopted him and gave him his name. He loves marmalade sandwiches.

2 I also felt the fact that the marmalade was golden was a confirmation that it was from God and it was a *'Golden opportunity'!*

LIFESTYLE

WALKING + TALKING IN EVERYDAY CONNECTION WITH JESUS

We've thought about how God loves to speak *to* us, and sometimes *through* us, to others. I've also mentioned, again and *again,* about how relationship is key.

But listening to and living with a God who walks and talks with us was always intended to be an ongoing lifestyle for us as ambassadors, representing Jesus wherever we go.

HE LOOKS
JUST LIKE
HIS FATHER!

HE LOOKS
JUST LIKE
HIS FATHER!

HE LOOKS
JUST LIKE
HIS FATHER!

HE LOOKS
JUST LIKE
HIS FATHER!

HE LOOKS
JUST LIKE
HIS FATHER!

HE LOOKS
JUST LIKE
HIS FATHER!

HE LOOKS
JUST LIKE
HIS FATHER!

HE LOOKS
JUST LIKE
HIS FATHER!

HE LOOKS
JUST LIKE
HIS FATHER!

HE LOOKS
JUST LIKE
HIS FATHER!

HE LOOKS
JUST LIKE
HIS FATHER!

HE LOOKS
JUST LIKE
HIS FATHER!

HE LOOKS
JUST LIKE
HIS FATHER!

HE LOOKS
JUST LIKE
HIS FATHER!

HE LOOKS
JUST LIKE
HIS FATHER!

HE LOOKS
JUST LIKE
HIS FATHER!

HE LOOKS
JUST LIKE
HIS FATHER!

HE LOOKS
JUST LIKE
HIS FATHER!

HE LOOKS
JUST LIKE
HIS FATHER!

HE LOOKS
JUST LIKE
HIS FATHER!

ROYAL REPRESENTATIVES

WE ARE CHRIST'S BODY ON EARTH

"And we all, who with unveiled faces contemplate the Lord's glory, are being transformed into his image with ever-increasing glory"
2 Corinthians 3:18

If I had a penny for every time someone said, *"He looks just like his father!"* my pockets would be full. It's true. Both my sons look like my husband, but in different ways. It's not only about the shared genetics they have, it's also about the subtle behaviours they've picked up as they've grown up.

Jesus was the exact representation of The Father.[1] As Christians, Jesus comes to live in us by His Spirit and we are being transformed to be more and more like *Him* every day.

According to the Joshua Project, approximately 7,000-people groups have no indigenous community of believing Christians able to evangelise to the rest of their people group. More than 42% of the world's population live in these 7,000-people groups.[2] We may assume that everyone knows who Jesus is, but that is incorrect. Many people do not.

As we live our everyday life, we will be meeting people who don't yet know Jesus, but who Jesus wants to connect with. Our job as ambassadors is to show others what Jesus looks and sounds like as we live in ongoing connection with Him.

We get to *represent* and *reveal* Jesus in everything we do. This is a great honour and responsibility!

IDEA – REFLECT

Whatever ground we stand on becomes the place we represent Jesus and His Kingdom.

Our representation of Him needs to be accurate!

1 Hebrews 1:3

2 https://joshuaproject.net/resources/articles/has_everyone_heard

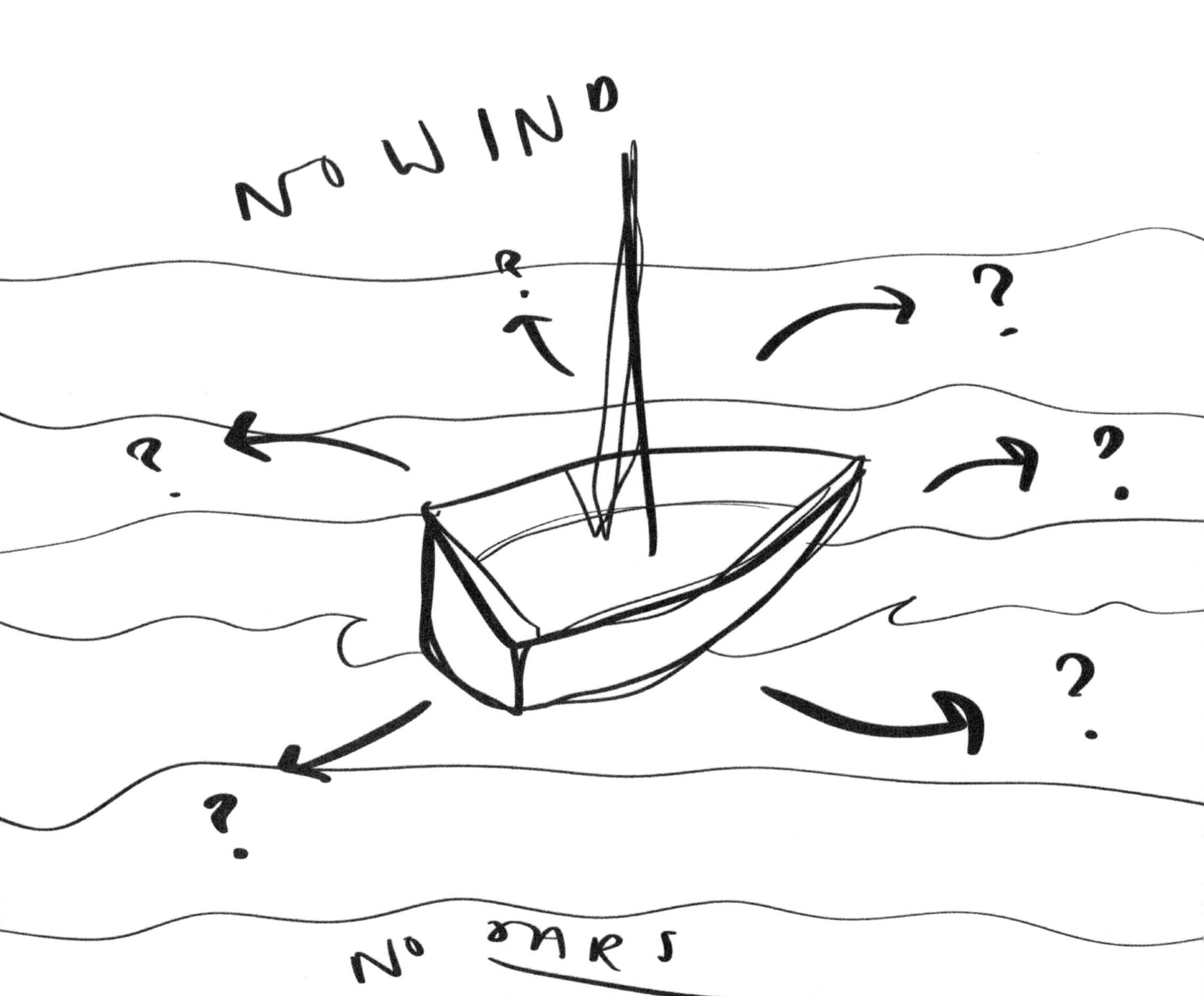
NO WIND
NO OARS

SPIRIT-FILLED

WE NEED GOD'S POWER & PRESENCE

"In a few days you will be baptised with the Holy Spirit."
Acts 1:4

If you're on a boat without oars and there's no wind, how will you sail? If you're in a hot air balloon and there's no fire, how will you fly? If you're on a train, but there's no electricity, how will you move?

Just before Jesus ascended into heaven, He told His disciples to wait and not do anything until they'd been filled with the Holy Spirit. He knew that in order for them to do all the things that He'd asked them to do,[1] they needed the Spirt's help in an essential, ongoing, everyday way.

As Christ's ambassadors, this applies to us as well. Acts 1:8 says: *"You will receive power when the Holy Spirit comes on you."* We need the Spirit's power to live the life that He intends us to live.

In Acts 2:4, we can read what happened when the disciples were filled with the Spirit: *"All of them were filled with the Holy Spirit and began to speak in other tongues as the Spirit enabled them."*

The gift of tongues (or 'languages') is an extremely powerful gift.[2] I once challenged myself to pray with my heavenly language for an hour every day for a month. I wanted to see whether it made any difference to what and how I prayed! As I carried out this little experiment I found it was like having the eyes of my heart sharpened and refocused.[3] I knew and connected to God's heart in a different way. I now use this gift as much as possible.

IDEA – DO

If you haven't been baptised with the Holy Spirit, then ask God to fill you!

---

1 Which included: *"Heal the sick, raise the dead, cleanse those who have leprosy, drive out demons."* Matthew 10:8

2 A gift of the Spirit that involves speaking in a heavenly language that hasn't been learnt (see 1 Corinthians 14). Although many get the gift when they're first filled with the Spirit, I had to keep asking for it before I actually got it!

3 1 Corinthians 14:4 (NLT) says: *"A person who speaks in tongues is strengthened personally."* This was what I was experiencing.

BUSY BUSY BUSY

BUSY

BUSY

BUSY BUSY BUSY

BUSY BUSY

BUSY BUSY BUSY

BUSY BUSY

BUSY BUSY BUSY

BUSY BUSY BUSY

BUSY BUSY BUSY

BUSY BUSY

BUSY BUSY BUSY

BUSY

WE MIGHT MISS GOD

BUSY BUSY BUSY

BUSY BUSY BUSY

ON THE WAY

GIVE GOD ROOM TO ADD HIS SURPRISES

"As Jesus was on his way, the crowds almost crushed him. And a woman was there who had been subject to bleeding for twelve years, but no one could heal her. She came up behind him and touched the edge of his cloak, and immediately her bleeding stopped."
Luke 8:41-45

If you read through the Gospels you'll see that Jesus has so many significant encounters with people whilst He was on His way somewhere. On His way to Jairus' house, Jesus heals a woman and stops to talk to her. He knew that going to Jairus' sick daughter was not the primary focus of the Father in that very moment. The woman in front of Him was.

I always used to plan to arrive somewhere exactly on time. For example, I knew the school run took me exactly eight minutes to walk at a brisk pace, so I'd leave with exactly eight minutes to go.

One day, I passed a very distressed woman at the bus stop. She needed the bus to come soon otherwise she'd miss her hospital appointment. I felt great compassion for her and that I should pray with her. However, I also knew that if I stopped to pray, I would be late to pick up my children. This unscheduled interaction was not factored into my eight-minute brisk walk! I had left no room for God to use me along the way.

So I left. And I didn't pray for her. As I walked away, I felt a great sadness in my heart. Here was an opportunity to share the Father's love with someone and because I had not given Him the room to do so, I had walked away.

If we leave no gaps in our lives for God's surprises, we'll limit how much He can use us.

IDEA – REFLECT

If we want God to use us, we must leave room for the unexpected.

FLEXIBLE

FLEXIBLE & EXPECTANT

GOD USES THOSE WHO ARE WILLING & AVAILABLE

"Then I heard the voice of the Lord saying, 'Whom shall I send? And who will go for us?' And I said, 'Here am I. Send me!'"

Isaiah 6:8

When skyscrapers are built in earthquake-prone areas, they're designed to be flexible. Structures that are too rigid with no room for movement collapse and crumble when an earthquake hits.

As God's ambassadors, we need to be lightweight, available and flexible. If our lives are too rigid then when God says, *"Whom shall I send?"* we aren't able to say, *"Send me!"* because we can't afford the flexibility.

Leviticus 23:22 says: *"When you reap the harvest of your land, do not reap to the very edges of your field or gather the gleanings of your harvest."*

This passage is about making sure that the poor were provided for during harvest time, but it carries an important principle. In our lives, do we leave margins or do we 'reap' right to the edges of our time, space and emotional resources?

The common response whenever I ask people how they are doing is: "I'm so busy!" What if we're more busy than God wants us to be? What if our lives are so full that there's no room for God to take us on detours, to do the stuff that He really wants us to be doing? What would happen if we intentionally left room in our day for God to show up and do something special, something different, to what we've planned?

IDEA – REFLECT

Busyness can rob us of the interactions God is wanting to give us.

Are you too busy?[1]

1 I always used to try to get my grocery shopping done as quickly as possible. However, I've learnt that sometimes God wants to speak to us as we shop and add to our list. One winter I felt God prompting me to pick up some gold chocolate coins as part of my grocery shop. I then felt Him tell me who to give them to along with the encouragement that God was going to take care of their financial needs. This turned out to be correct and the person later had the financial breakthrough that they'd been needing.

SMELLY LIVES

JESUS IN US STIRS A HUNGER IN OTHERS

"For we are to God the pleasing aroma of Christ among those who are being saved and those who are perishing."
2 Corinthians 2:15

I have a faithful, long-lasting relationship with coffee. I am also very committed to sleep. Sometimes in the morning when I'm fast asleep, the thing that awakens me is not the clatter and noise of the day, but the smell of freshly filtered coffee wafting its way upstairs, beckoning me out of the depths of my unconscious.

We are the aroma of Christ. That's what the passage we've just read says. Wherever we go, aware of it or not, we smell of Jesus. As we listen and respond to God's voice and direction in our every day life, we will be partnering with the Holy Spirit to awaken a deep hunger inside others to get to know Christ.

Sometimes people don't realise they're hungry... until they smell freshly baked bread. When we live freshly baked lives of ongoing connection with Jesus, other people will taste, see and smell that the Lord is good through you.[1] And it will leave them hungry for a taste of more.[2]

I recently noticed that my son didn't want to go to Sunday school any more; he just wanted to stay with me in the main service. So I asked him why. He said that a few Sundays before as a church we'd all started to sing in the Spirit. As he heard it, he knew this was something genuinely from God. He had tasted something of heaven and he wanted more.

He was hungry.

IDEA – PRAY

"Jesus, please help me to live my life in such a way that it makes people hungry to know you."

1 Psalm 34:8

2 Allowing us opportunity to introduce them to the Great Baker! *"Jesus declared, "I am the bread of life. Whoever comes to me will never go hungry, and whoever believes in me will never be thirsty."* John 6:35

my son
me

MOMENT GRABBERS

SEIZE EVERY OPPORTUNITY GOD GIVES YOU

"Always be prepared to give an answer to everyone who asks you to give the reason for the hope that you have."
1 Peter 3:15

I never should have done it.

When my eldest son was about three years old, I made the mistake of taking my son out of the supermarket trolley. He was restless and wanted to stretch his legs and didn't like being trapped in his little, restrictive seat. So I let him out. Before I could give him strict instructions about staying at my side at all times, he zoomed off as fast as his little legs could take him.

He was not wasting a second of his freedom.

As calmly and as quickly as I could, I searched the aisles looking high and low for him - under the shelving and behind the packaging. But then I spotted him and he was suspiciously still, even as he saw me approach. It soon became apparent why.

He had found the pick 'n mix section and his face was stuffed so full of sweets his lips couldn't close. He saw his moment and he seized it with both hands, literally.

Sometimes God will give us unexpected moments to share His heart with others that He will want us to boldly and courageously seize with both hands.

IDEA - PRAY

"Father, give me courage to make the most of every opportunity you give me." (Ephesians 5:16)

SIN

RADICAL HOLINESS

ZERO SIN TOLERANCE

"Let us throw off everything that hinders and the sin that so easily entangles. And let us run with perseverance the race marked out for us, fixing our eyes on Jesus, the pioneer and perfecter of faith."
Hebrews 12:1-2

Last year, Daniel and I visited some friends who'd just moved into a beautiful house built in the 1800s. During our stay, they explained to us how they'd had to spend thousands of pounds to have the entire house treated because there had been such a bad damp problem. Apparently, the previous owners had spotted a drip in the bathroom but never dealt with it. Over time, what began as a single drop ended up soaking the entire house, compromising its integrity.

This is the same with sin.

When we aren't *ruthless* about not tolerating those single drops of sin, they can cause serious damage.[1]

As God's ambassadors who can hear and share God's voice, we need to live outrageously holy lives! Part of this will involve giving permission to others to speak truth about ourselves, which may include things about our character that need to be dealt with. We need others to help us *"throw off everything that hinders and the sin that so easily entangles".*

We need to live radically holy lives.

IDEA – REFLECT

Is there anything that you need to repent of (say sorry and turn away from)?

God is gracious and quick to forgive.

---

1 I think this is a great quote: *"Never tolerate, because of sympathy for yourself or for others, any practice that is not in keeping with a holy God. Holiness means absolute purity of your walk before God, the words coming from your mouth, and every thought in your mind – placing every detail of your life under the scrutiny of God Himself."* Oswald Chambers

YOU ARE HERE

END OF THE BOOK

WILL YOU LET HIM IN?

AN ADVENTURE AWAITS

JESUS STANDS AT THE DOOR, KNOCKING

"Whether you turn to the right or to the left, your ears will hear a voice behind you, saying, 'This is the way; walk in it.'"

Isaiah 30:21

You've made it to the end - well done!

I hope that as we've journeyed together you've had a little glimpse of what a life of walking with Jesus can look like. This has been part of my story. Now it's your turn.

Jesus wants to write that story with you.

He was right next to you as you read every page. He's now looking for what you'll do next and how you will respond.

An adventure awaits you. Jesus is knocking. Will you let Him in?

"Here I am! I stand at the door and knock. If anyone hears my voice and opens the door, I will come in and eat with that person, and they with me."

Revelation 3:20

ANNA GOODMAN

ASHLEY DREW

ABOUT US

WHO WE ARE

ANNA GOODMAN

Anna was born in Honduras and is married to Daniel, who was born in Guinea Bissau, West Africa. Anna has also lived in Nepal, Belgium and Barbados. Her maternal grandmother was Swiss and she has Croatian and Swedish sisters-in-law. Both her parents are British. Anna now lives in Cambridge, which is both very international and very British at the same time - much like her heart!

Anna moved to the UK in 1996 to do her A-levels and then went to the University of St. Andrews, Scotland, to do a neuroscience degree. In 2002, she moved down to Cambridge to complete a PhD, which is when she met Daniel who now leads the church they attend.

The first time Anna can remember hearing from God was when she was eight years old. She's therefore a big believer that you're never too young to hear God's voice. She is currently focusing on raising her two young sons to grow up listening and responding to God's voice for themselves.

Blog and website: annagoodman.co.uk
Instagram: @annagoodman_writer
Twitter: @Goodman_Anna

ASHLEY DREW

Ashley grew up in the wonderful city of Norwich. She spent most of her childhood drawing anywhere and everywhere, being creative (which was often very messy), reading many, many books and playing imaginative games. Ashley attempted to escape from Norwich, but, after three and a half years away, has found herself back in Norfolk!

Ashley studied graphic design at Coventry University and spent three years falling more in love with hand-lettering and illustration. She loves the challenge of helping people understand complex ideas and concepts through her work.

In 2019, Ashley moved to Cambridge for ID, (Intentional Discipleship, a Relational Mission year out) and spent a year intentionally pursuing God, serving the church and getting to know Anna... which is how Ashley ended up being asked to illustrate this very book. God has done more than she could have asked or imagined with her year so far!

Website: ashleydrew.co.uk
Instagram: @ashleyjdrew

THANK YOU

There are so many people I could thank, it's hard to know where to start and when to stop. In the spirit of keeping things concise, I will keep it short.

To my biological and spiritual parents - Marcus, Gilli, Tony, Sue, Katie, Valerie, Angela, Ginny and Mike. You have intentionally watered, pruned and shaped me in many different ways. I am forever grateful.

Daniel, I couldn't have done this without you. Thank you for always keeping me grounded in the Gospel.

Ashley, thank you for being part of this particular adventure and for bringing my words alive.

Dave, thank you for all your “;x(‘.,.<.?!”1-[2]*^>” skills.

Lynn and Lucy - you are prayer warriors who know the power of words. Thank you for your amazing support.

And thank you to Frank the slug for bringing us joy.

Anna

With the fear of being told off by Anna for not being conscise - I too shall also keep this short!

To my wonderful parents for always encouraging my creativity (and for putting up with the trail of pencil sharpenings, paint splodges, carpet stains, and 1000's of sheets of printing).

Anna, thank you for inviting me join you on this adventure.

Ashley

Printed in Great Britain
by Amazon

62043113R00140